50¢ 55

D0886836

———— ※ ————

TEN RULES
FOR LIVING

BOOKS BY THE SAME AUTHOR

TEN RULES
FOR LIVING

CLOVIS G. CHAPPELL

ABINGDON PRESS
NEW YORK • NASHVILLE

TEN RULES FOR LIVING

Copyright MCMXXXVIII by Whitmore & Smith

J

SET UP, PRINTED, AND BOUND BY THE
PARTHENON PRESS, AT NASHVILLE,
TENNESSEE, UNITED STATES OF AMERICA

38,792

TO MY SONS
CLOVIS JUNIOR
AND ROBERT

whose unfailing loyalty
has helped me preach without apology and without
embarrassment

CONTENTS

7

TEN RULES
FOR LIVING

I

BEGIN WITH GOD

Thou shalt have no other gods before me.

EXODUS 20: 3

THIS EVENING WE ARE BEGINNING A STUDY OF that ancient code known as The Ten Commandments. I have called these old laws Ten Rules for Living. By this, I do not mean that they speak the final word on human conduct. I am not forgetting that Jesus summed up these ten words in the one law of love: "Thou shalt love the Lord thy God with all thy heart, and with all thy soul, and with all thy mind, and with all thy strength, . . . and thy neighbor as thyself." But in this day when so many are confused, when so many seem to have flung away from their old convictions and let go their moorings, I am wondering if these rules might not serve as guideposts to finer and fuller living.

Naturally, there are those who do not believe that this is the case. They are sure that this ancient code is fit for nothing but the wastebasket. There is a story of a certain master and slave who years ago went deep-sea fishing. When they were making their way back to shore late in the night, the master became sleepy and turned the helm over to his faithful servant, Mose. Before doing this, however, he pointed out the north star to Mose and urged him to keep his eye on it. But the master had not been asleep very long before Mose snatched forty winks himself. When he awakened he was in utter confusion. He called his master frantically. "Wake up!" he said, "and show me another star. I've done run clean past that one!"

So many feel about these ten commandments. But it is my conviction that we can no more run past this ancient code than we can run past the north star. These laws are not merely arbitrary rules like the one that compels us to drive on the right side of the street rather than on the left. They partake of the nature of principles. I am quite sure that Einstein does not begin each day by a recitation of the multiplication table. Yet, great mathematician that he is, he can never ignore the fact that twice two make four without utter confusion. Our modern scientists do not rush to the apple orchard each morning to have confirmed to them the reality of the law of gravitation. Yet they cannot ignore that law without disaster. The same is true of this ancient code. To violate it brings disaster to the individual and to society as a whole. To observe it is to plant our feet on the road to a fuller individual and social life.

I

LET us look now at this first commandment. Very appropriately it begins with God. That is always the best place to begin. This first commandment has a brief preface. "I am the Lord thy God. . . . Thou shalt have no other gods before me." This code, you see, begins with a great assumption. It assumes the reality of God. It begins by asserting that God is. The author of this code, whoever he may have been, makes no effort to prove God. He simply affirms him. In so doing, he is in harmony with all the other writers of the Bible. The psalmists do not argue about God. They realize Him and rejoice in His mercies. The prophets never undertake to prove God; they proclaim Him. This is emphatically true of Jesus. He lived in constant fellowship with the Father. He communed with him; he did his work through the might of his

13

power. He revealed him, saying, "He that hath seen me hath seen the Father." But he never argued about Him.

These psalmists and prophets do not take this position, I am sure, because there are no evidences of God. Of course, we cannot prove God by any sort of logic; yet there are unmistakable evidences of his existence. This ordered universe with its infinite marks of intelligence is one tremendous evidence. If you tell me that you drive a car, and I ask you what make it is, I feel that I am asking a perfectly reasonable question. If you answer, "It is no make at all; it is the result of blind forces that had no pre-vision of what they were creating," I will not conclude that you are wiser than I, but only that you are less sane. With the poet, we can still hear God say:

"Before the roaring loom of time I ply,
And weave the garment thou seest me by."

But far more convincing than this ordered universe is man himself. There is a sense in which man has seemed to grow less significant in the light of the infinite ages that this universe has existed. He seems to have grown less significant also as its walls have been pushed back to infinite bounds. Yet neither age nor size is a supreme badge of greatness. Man is far greater than his universe because he can contemplate it; he can bridge its rivers; he can measure its suns; he can weigh its stars; he can do what the vastest of its planets cannot do—he can think, and will, and love.

The chief reason, I think, that these great spiritual leaders do not deal with evidences is, first of all, because they realize that all evidences are in a sense inadequate. When I was a boy it was the custom, when there was company, for children to wait and eat at the second table. Of course, we were allowed to sop the skillet and eat the neck of the chicken, but that was about all. At times, when this company was more numerous than was expected, I have gone into dinner to find unmistakable evidence of fried chicken. There were bones in every plate, but though there were evidences, there was little else.

Some one of you, perchance, has an old rose pressed away in a book. When you look at it you are reminded of one that plucked and gave it to you years ago, when love's morning had its dawn. It is an evidence of one that you have loved and lost, but it is a poor substitute. There are two little baby shoes that you have tucked away in the dresser drawer. They remind you of a little baby that once hugged your neck and kissed your lips. They are evidences of the baby that toddled out of your arms and out of your world, but could never get out of your heart. But though these shoes are evidences, they are poor substitutes for the baby himself.

Then, I think, these discoverers in the realm of the spiritual do not greatly concern themselves with evidences because they have something so much better to offer. They see little use of arguing about the reality and usefulness of bread when a table is spread in their very midst. It seems to them a matter of second-rate importance to argue with thirsty men and women about the reality of water, when in their very presence there is a gushing spring waiting to be kissed upon its sparkling lips. Thus they are more or less indifferent to evidences because they are so sure that they have something far better to offer. They have God himself.

II

THAT God is available is the assertion of this first law. "I am the Lord thy God. . . . Thou shalt have no other gods before me." That is, God is not only a reality, but he is a reality that is accessible. He is available for human need. I may fall at his feet, if I will, and say with Thomas, "My Lord, and my God." I may shout with the victorious certainty of St. Paul, "My God shall supply every need of yours according to his riches in glory by Christ Jesus." Every man, asserts this ancient law, may have God for his very own.

Of course, the conception of God that was prevalent when this code was written is not our conception. Man's conception of God has changed vastly since then. Since then, the Word has become flesh and dwelt among us, and we have been privileged to behold his glory. We have seen him gather little children into his arms. We have seen him bend over outcasts in love and mercy. We have seen him make every man's burden his own. We have heard him say, "If God were here he would be doing just what I am doing. He is here in me, for he that hath seen me hath seen the Father."

But the fact that our conceptions of God change with the passing of the years does not mean that God changes. Our conception of the universe has changed vastly since that far-off day. Their universe was a very small affair; ours stretches away into the infinite. When the psalmist sang, "When I consider thy heavens, the work of thy fingers, the moon and the stars which thou hast ordained, what is man that thou art mindful of him?" he thought of those stars and of that moon as very near and friendly little candles to light his way. We think of them today in a far different fashion. Yet they are the very same stars and the very same moon at which the psalmist looked. In the same way, though our conceptions of God change, God abides, "the same yesterday, today, and forever."

Now in saying that God is ours for the taking, this ancient lawgiver speaks in harmony with the whole Bible. This affirmation that sounds hearteningly in the Old Testament rises to a shout of victory in the New. Whatever else we may miss, no man need miss God. How insistent and appealing is this declaration upon the lips of Jesus! In that marvelous story of the perfect father that he tells us in the fifteenth chapter of St. Luke, there is one son that remains dutifully at home. "Now the elder son was in the field." That tells of a clean environment. He was out where the skies were blue over his head. He was out where he could get the fragrance of the upturned sod and the sweet aroma of the new-mown hay. The word also speaks of toil. He was a worker, while his brother was a waster. But when he told his experience, it was distressingly disappointing. He had not lived as a son at all, but

only as a slave. "All these years do I slave for thee
... and thou never gavest me a kid to make merry
with my friends." And his father does not deny
the truth of this. But over against his dismal experience he puts what might have been. "Son, thou
art ever with me, and all that I have is thine."

III

Now, since God is available, how are we to come
into the richness of our inheritance? How may we
come to possess God and be possessed by him?

In order to possess God, we must meet certain
conditions. That is just plain common sense.
"There is gold in those hills," we are accustomed to
say. But before that gold becomes ours it must
be mined. There is learning to be had from books.
"Reading makes a full man." But those books
must be read before the knowledge they contain
becomes ours. When I was a youth I undertook to
play the violin. It was a futile effort. The queer
and horrid noises that I made would never have
passed for music, even in an age of jazz. Had I
had only my experience to go by, I should have said,
"There is no music in the violin." Indeed, there was
not for me, because I failed to meet the conditions.
But the same could not be said of this instrument in

the hands of Fritz Kreisler. How silly it would be for me to declare the violin tuneless after my half-hearted effort of an hour! Yet there are those who treat God in this fashion, though they have scarcely given him as much attention as I gave my violin. If we find God, certain conditions must be met.

Some of us fail to meet these conditions because we are preoccupied. In a conversation with a friend some time ago, I put this question to him: "How can you ignore the fact of God as you do?" He was an honest man. He answered frankly, "I keep busy. I do not allow myself to think about God." There are those who, like the guest invited to the wedding feast, are too interested in land and oxen, in the newly married wife, to have any time for God. Naturally, they fail to find him. We do not come to possess any prize by simply ignoring it.

Then, there are those who get rid of God by wishful thinking. Of course, to know God is the supremest of privileges. It is this knowledge that, above all else, brings to us inward strength. To know him is to have poise, it is to have serenity, it is to have courage. It is to be, as another has put it, absurdly joyful. It is to have an outgoing love, a good will that is at once aggressive and sacrificial. Possessing God, we do possess all things. But in spite of this, there are those to whom he is no more than an embarrassment.

This is the case because the fact of God not only brings great privileges, but also tremendous responsibilities. While it is the highest of all privileges to be his sons, we, of course, cannot avoid the obligations that result from sonship to such a father. If we have God, for instance, we have an eternity on our hands. We have to live with ourselves through endless ages. That fact brings us into an altitude where some of us find the breathing a bit difficult. That was the case with the fool of whom the psalmist wrote. This fool found God a bit annoying. He disturbed him by calling him to a type of life that was beyond his gallantry and grit. Therefore, he decided to dismiss him. "The fool hath said in his heart, there is no God." He determined to act as if God were a lie, and to him, so acting, God did become a lie.

If, then, there are conditions of possessing God and being possessed by him, what are these conditions? We find the answer in germ here in this ancient law. Of course, the way is made more clear in the New Testament. But, even here, we find enough light, if we but follow it, to bring us into the fullness of the light. "Thou shalt have no other gods before me." Positively stated, it would read like this: "If thou wilt let all other gods go, then thou shalt have me." There is a saying that when the half-gods go, the gods arrive. Certainly it is true that when our lesser gods go, God himself arrives. That is, we find God when we are willing to give up all else in order to find him. These ancient Jews could have the God of Israel only as they were willing to let the gods of the surrounding nations go.

We of today do not believe in these lesser gods. But in spite of that fact, we are as truly polytheists as they. We no longer think of Mars as a person, but we worship the things for which he stood with the same loyal devotion of those of the long ago. We no longer bow at the shrine of Venus, but that for which Venus stood still lays its enslaving and defiling hand on millions. We would never dream of worshipping Bacchus, the god of drink and revelry, as a person. But perhaps he has never been shone greater respect, nor had more willing worshipers, than in wet America today.

A few weeks ago the Chamber of Commerce in the city of Dayton, Ohio, made an investigation as to how the people of that city were spending their money. They found the following startling facts.

The citizens of Dayton were spending $113,000 more each week for liquor than for groceries. Now everybody in Dayton has to eat, but everybody does not have to drink. Yet those who drink spend the bulk of the money. The *Central Christian Advocate* makes this amazing statement: "Since 1933 those on relief, those who are being supported by the money of the taxpayers, have spent three billions of dollars for liquor." Yes, our old gods are still with us, and we still worship them with the same fervor as did those of the long ago.

But here stands this ancient lawgiver saying, "If you will give up these lesser gods, you may have the real God." Jesus was saying the same thing in a clearer fashion when he declared, "If any man is willing to do His will, he shall know." There is a roadway to spiritual certainty. That is the road of the surrendered life. I have said it before, I cannot say it too often—if you will begin here and now to do the will of God as best you know that will, if you will begin here and now to walk the road that you believe God wants you to walk, sooner or later you will encounter Him upon that road, and you will be able to say, "My Lord and my God."

How strikingly this is shown in that beautiful story, "The Man That Played God." A great musician was playing for royalty one night, when a bomb was thrown in an effort to kill the king. The king was not hurt, but the explosion plunged the musician into utter silence. He never heard again. He had to give up his career. He came back to New York City in bitterness and brokenness of heart. One day when an old friend came to see him, he took down the New Testament and read to this friend a passage that had once been his favorite, "Are not two sparrows sold for a farthing, yet not one of them is forgotten before God." "It is not true," said the great artist savagely. "God does not love like that, or he would not have allowed me to be robbed of all that I hold dear."

By and by this deaf musician was induced to learn lip-reading. He lived in a flat that overlooked Central Park. He began to amuse himself, little by little, by watching through his field glasses the pageantry of life that passed beneath his windows. One day he saw a frail young man, with a girl on his arm, come into the park. He read the lips of this young man as he told the girl he loved how he had just been to his physician, and had been sentenced to death. "I have tuberculosis. But I could be cured," he said desperately, "if I could only go to the mountains. But that would take a thousand dollars, and I have almost nothing." Then he lifted his face to the heights, and prayed for a chance to live. The great artist heard that prayer, and at once sent his valet with a check for the money.

This experience brought such joy to the giver that he began to watch more closely, and with increasing interest, the procession of sorrowing and burdened men and women that came within his view. More and more he forgot himself as he took their burdens and their needs upon his own shoulders. At last, as he walked this roadway of sacrificial service, God dawned upon him like the slow breaking of a radiant day. Doing the will of God, he came to know him. So it may be with you and me. He surrounds us as the atmosphere. He is standing even now at the door of our hearts. He is knocking as he woos us with this tender appeal: "If any man will open the door, I will come in and sup with him and he with me." This means that if we are willing to give up our lesser gods, we shall know the real God. Thus this commandment becomes to us not merely a forbidding law, but a radiant gospel.

II

KEEP YOUR EYE ON THE GOAL

Thou shalt not make unto thee any graven image, or any likeness of any thing that is in heaven above, or that is in the earth beneath, or that is in the water under the earth: Thou shalt not bow down thyself to them, nor serve them: for I the Lord thy God am a jealous God, visiting the iniquity of the fathers upon the children unto the third and fourth generation of them that hate me; and showing mercy unto thousands of them that love me, and keep my commandments.

EXODUS 20: 4-6

I

"THOU SHALT NOT MAKE UNTO THEE ANY graven image." As it stands, nothing could be further removed from our modern life than this command. Who of us feels a pang of conscience in its presence? Who of us is made to smite himself upon the breast, and cry, "God be merciful to me a

26

sinner"? Frankly, the temptation to make images has never troubled me in the least. In fact, the making of any kind of picture has never been to me a major temptation. Some time ago a small boy with whom I was trying to get on good terms asked me to draw him a mule. Now such an undertaking should have been easy. The mule and I are old friends; we grew up together. But though I gave to the undertaking my best skill, when I showed the finished product to the ungrateful rascal, he burst into tears. Naturally, therefore, this second rule for living leaves me cold.

But this is the case, not because this command really has nothing to say to me. It is rather the case because I am looking at its outer surface instead of its inner meaning. Naturally, this rule requires some explaining. We need to see how it came to be. To find the answer to this question we must ask another, and that is this: how did men come to make images of their god or gods after the fashion that is here forbidden? What lay behind the whole image-making business?

The answer to this question is quite evident. We may be sure at once that those who first made images of their gods were not doing so in order either to destroy or to degrade religion. They had a purpose in view in the making of these images that was altogether worthy. Primitive man naturally found it hard to realize a god or gods that he could not see. When he prayed, he too often felt that he was praying into space, that he was uttering words into the ear of mere nothingness. He made him an image, therefore, to assist his sluggish imagination. He was earnestly trying in this fashion to bring a sense of reality into his worship.

The need of visible helps in worship has not been felt by primitive man alone. People have made use of the visible in order to make more real the Invisible all through the centuries. Our Catholic friends do so to this day. And we are not going to deny that some of them are greatly benefited thereby. Frank Boreham tells of a certain lovely saint who had the habit of setting a vacant chair before him every time he prayed. When this man explained his reason, he told the following story: Years before he had complained to his pastor that he found great difficulty in realizing that God was present and listening. Therefore his pastor told him to set a chair before him, and to imagine that his Lord was sitting in it, as he surely would be. He found the practice so helpful that he kept it up through the years. One night he slipped away while others slept.

But in the morning, when they found his cold hand resting upon the chair that he had set for his Master, they knew that he had not died alone.

The images that these ancient people made in order to help them to worship were, perhaps, of real assistance for a time. But in the end, they became a hindrance and a snare. This was the case because, little by little, the worshipers came so to fix their gaze upon the image that they forgot the one that was imaged. They became so absorbed in the means that they forgot the end, so concerned in the picture that they lost sight of the reality. They were so intent upon that which was to help them to realize God that they lost God altogether. It was as if this old Scottish saint whose story we have just told had come to look solely at the chair that he set for his Lord rather than at the Master that his devout imagination pictured as occupying that chair.

II

THE temptation thus to take our eyes off the goal, and to confuse the means with the end, is one that haunts us in every department of life. This rule, therefore, ceases to be a dead law of a long dead past. It becomes rather an abiding principle that will be just as applicable ten thousand years from today as it is at this present moment. How persistent is this temptation thus to take our eyes off the goal! It belongs not merely to today, but to every day.

1. Take the matter of eating and drinking, for instance. These are, of course, absolutely necessary to physical life. "Man shall not live by bread alone," Jesus said. That is profoundly true. But it is also equally true that he cannot live without bread. We have had a recent example of a certain minister over in Tennessee that undertook to do so. He was going to put on the Godhead bodily. But what he was really putting on was not the Godhead, but his own shroud. Had friends not interfered, he would have gone posthaste to the cemetery. All this he would have suffered for the innocent resolve of refusing to eat.

But while we must eat in order to live, we need to bear in mind that eating is a means to an end, and not an end in itself. It is wise to eat to live, but it is foolish and deadly to live to eat. But thousands are doing just that. One of my stewards told me of taking a mutual friend of ours to lunch some time ago. This friend ate his principal meal in the evening. Therefore, all he ate for lunch was seventy-two oysters. That modest meal was quite enough for twelve ordinary men. No wonder that, thus digging his grave with his teeth, he passed prematurely to his reward. Eating as a means is sane and sensible. To refuse to do so is silly and suicidal. But eating as an end is at once foolish, gluttonous, and deadly.

2. Then there is the matter of recreation. Everybody needs to enjoy some kind of pastime. All work and no play does really make Jack a dull boy. But all play and no work inflicts upon Jack a greater penalty even than dullness. There are those whose one purpose in life seems to be to have a good time. These believe so strongly in their pleasures that they make them an end in themselves. They live in order to find thrills. They demand of every experience that it pack some sort of punch. But those taking this course make a twofold blunder. First, they fail to find the good time for which they seek. When joy is sought as an end, it always eludes us. Second, when a good time becomes an end, what was meant to be a recreation becomes a dissipation.

Here, I take it, is one of the sanest tests both of what pleasures and pastimes are legitimate, and of the place we are to give them in our lives. Of course we do not look on pleasure as sinful in itself. We believe, as another has said, that no pleasure is sinful except sinful pleasure. But only that recreation

31

is legitimate that is of such quality and quantity as to re-create. If after your play, whatever it is, you have a better body, a clearer head, and a finer fitness for your task, you are on the right road. But if after your play, you find yourself less fit, the chances are great that you are on a wrong road. What you sought as recreation has become a dissipation. This means that you have failed to keep your eye on the goal, and have substituted the means for the end.

3. Then there is the matter of making money. There has been quite a bit of foolish talk in recent days about money-making. Some have sneered at it as if it were a base and ignoble achievement. This has been the case in spite of the fact that all of us have been willing to use some bit of it, however much we may have scorned the sordid task of making it. But to throw off on money-making as an evil in itself is pure cant. It is perfectly right to make money if we do it in an ethical way. There is no necessary virtue in merely being penniless. There used to be a worthless old loafer in our village, when I was a boy, whose one contribution was this bit of wisdom: "I had rather be a poor man and go to heaven than to be a rich man and go to hell." But I have never been sure that his ability to live off

the toil of others got him through the pearly gates. I fancy he would have stood a better chance if, by honest sweat, he had made a little money.

This is the case because money, rightly made and rightly used, may be a source of endless good. How often we hear someone misquote Paul by saying, "Money is the root of all evil." Paul said no such thing. He had far too much intelligence to say anything so silly. Money can feed the hungry and clothe the naked. Money can build schools, colleges, and universities. Money can erect churches to the glory of God. I know that I can take a dollar and use it in such a fashion as to make the eagle upon it turn vulture to tear at somebody's heart. But I can also take that same dollar and so use it that the eagle upon it will become a mockingbird to make music in somebody's soul. Money rightly used is a means of endless good.

But while money is vastly useful when employed as a means, it is frightfully deadly when we make it an end. While it is genuinely helpful as a servant, it can be a perfectly hellish master. Therefore Paul said that the love of money is the root of every kind of evil. And this is true. How few men can make money rapidly and remain Christian! Money tends to do two things to us: to give us a false in-

33

dependence, and to absorb our interest. After watching its influence on men for a good many years, I am convinced that the love of it kills about as many men as liquor. When men cease to use it as a means to an end and make it an end in itself, nothing can be more deadly.

In one of McGuffey's readers there is a story of a miser who had under his basement a subbasement that was known only to himself. Here he kept his silver and his gold. Here he would come secretly to worship. It was his custom to run his bony fingers through the coins and listen to the music of their clank, as he said, "O my Beauties, O my Beauties!" But one day, while he was thus worshiping, a vagrant wind blew the door of the subbasement shut. It fastened with a spring lock that could only be turned from the outside. Thus the miser was shut in with his gold. Years later, when men tore down his old house, they found a skeleton draped over a heap of coins. He had taken money and made it his god, and that god had destroyed him. But money was no more deadly for him than it is for those who, today, change it from a means into an end.

4. What a fine something is popularity! Recently a man wrote a delightful book entitled *How to*

Make Friends and Influence People. He points out the way to popularity. In so doing, he has rendered a service. We could all be more popular than we are. And because we could be we ought to be. Recently I went to hear a friend speak to a group of students. He began by taking a bit of money from his pocket, saying, "I always empty my pockets before going to bed. Following this practice the other night, I took out a half dollar, a quarter, a nickel, and two pennies. Now you know," he continued, "that money talks. Therefore, this half dollar began at once to talk to me. 'Why are you not popular?' it questioned. 'Take me, for example; I am popular because I am a democrat. For days I have been associating with these lesser coins, but not once have I lorded it over them. I have been a thorough democrat; therefore I am popular.' "

Now popularity is something to be desired. A certain measure of it is necessary to our highest usefulness. Take my own calling, for instance. Before one can render any great service as a minister, he must have a measure of popularity. Though he may speak with the tongue of men and of angels, if his hearers dislike him he can do little for them. They simply shrug their shoulders and say, "I don't like him anyway." So saying, they go away unhelped. But if people like the minister, then almost any sermon is good; he can say anything that ought to be said and get away with it. If not, the most trifling thing will offend. The measure of his ability to help, therefore, is partly the measure of his popularity.

Since this is the case, the desire to be popular is a perfectly normal and wholesome desire. But, even so, we can give it a place in our thinking and in our striving far beyond what it deserves. As a means to an end, it is good and worth while. But as an end in itself, it is not only unworthy, but hurtful. My friend, in pursuing his parable, remarked that while this half dollar did emphasize the importance of popularity, it did not make it of supreme importance. Therefore it continued after this fashion: "While I have tried to be popular, I have not been so eager to do so that I have compromised. Though associating with lesser coins, I have continued to be worth my face value. I have never degenerated into a quarter, nor looked like two cents." Popularity is good as a means, but to make it an end is dangerous.

III

Now this temptation to take our eyes off the goal

and thus substitute the end for the means haunts us especially in the matters of religion.

1. Take the Bible, for instance. I confess to a deep love for this inspired and inspiring Book. It speaks home to my heart as no other book in all the world. There are countless others who can say a hearty amen to this declaration. But some, in their zeal, tend to make the Bible an end inself, instead of a means to an end. Jesus rebuked such in his day. "Ye search the Scriptures," he said, "because in them ye think ye have eternal life, but these are they that testify of me." The supreme value of the Bible is that it helps one to see God. "Beyond the sacred page I seek thee, Lord. My spirit pants for thee, O Living Word." The Bible, as another has said, ought to be used somewhat as we use a telescope. Here is a wonderful instrument that can bring far things near. But we may merely make a toy of it. We may open it out and shut it up and use it only to look at. But if we are wise we shall use it, not to look at, but to look through. So it is with the Bible. It is not an end in itself, but a means to an end. It is to bring us to a fuller vision.

2. Then there is the matter of joining the church. Mark me! I am a firm believer in joining some

church. I believe that this is not only every man's privilege, but also every man's obligation. The church is making a contribution to the community and to the world that is of supreme importance. The church furnishes that saving salt without which civilization rots down. Therefore, it is one's big opportunity to be a part of the salt instead of the rottenness, by being a worthy member of some church. If one is so cranky and cross-grained that one cannot unite in work and worship with any other group—that in itself is an indication that there is something desperately wrong. No man has a right, in a world like ours, to ignore the church and refuse to identify himself with it.

But though this is the case, we need to remind ourselves that joining the church is not an end in itself. No more is this the case when one joins a lodge or a civic club. I knew a man some time ago who joined the Masons, but he never went back after his initiation. Too often that is approximately the way some treat the church. Having stood at her altars and taken upon themselves her solemn vows, they go their indifferent ways as if all their obligations had been met. How wickedly absurd! Joining the church is good, but it is not an end in itself. It is only an enlistment; the fight is to come after. If we forget this, we have taken our eyes off the goal and headed toward disaster.

3. Not only is this true of joining the church, but of our whole relationship to the church and its work after joining. It is a duty and a privilege to attend the services of the church. To fail to do so is to become a hindrance rather than a help. But though attending church is important, it is not an end in itself. When it becomes an end, it becomes a menace and a snare. The same is true of giving. It is true of teaching; it is true of preaching. This is all a means to an end. And that end is the winning of men to Christ and the building of them up in Christ. That end, in short, is the bringing in of the Kingdom of God. For a minister to make a sermon an end in itself is to violate this commandment. When a certain pastor was persistently putting the few members in his congregation to sleep by preaching to the man in the moon, he explained his failure by saying that he could not compromise his literary style. As well might a surgeon become so concerned with the technique of his operation that he should no longer care about saving the life of his patient. Joining the church, then, and work in the church,

are not ends in themselves, but only a means to an end.

IV

To forget this second rule for living, therefore, spells disaster. Forgetfulness works disaster in one's own life. It works disaster in the lives of others. This rule reminds us that the sins of the fathers are visited on the children to the third and fourth generation. That is profoundly true. Our children are punished for our sins, or rather they are punished by them, even to the third and fourth generation. There is a terrible contagion about sin. Those parents that get so absorbed in the worship of mere means that they lose the real God out of their lives do rob their boys and girls and make life for them far more difficult.

But if the sins of the parents are visited upon the children, so also are their virtues. If sin is contagious, so is goodness. The reason that most of you are in this church is because you have been caught by the contagion of the nobly pure and saintly lives of your fathers and mothers. The reason that I am here is because it was my privilege to grow up in a home where first things were put first, where no lesser gods were allowed to take the place of Him whose nature and name is Love. It is the easier for all of us to keep our eyes upon the real goal of living because of the faithfulness of those who have gone before.

III

BE SINCERE

Thou shalt not take the name of the Lord thy God in vain; for the Lord will not hold him guiltless that taketh his name in vain.

EXODUS 20: 7

I

WHAT IS FORBIDDEN BY THIS COMMAND?

1. For a long time it has stood as the standard warning against profane swearing. Though this is not its primary purpose, it does, beyond question, forbid profanity. The habit of profanity is very common in our day. It experienced a tremendous revival during the World War. Multitudes, both men and women, became convinced that their vocabularies were so impoverished as to need to be enriched by profanity. They decided that their conversation would be disgustingly insipid unless

42

salted by vigorous, mouth-filling oaths. Therefore, they began to develop a proficiency in swearing that seems to have increased with the passing of years. Today profanity flavors much of our ordinary conversation and seems a vital part of our literature.

But in spite of its popularity, it is at once silly and vulgar. This does not mean that there are not highly intelligent men and women who are addicted to the habit of swearing. But it does mean that those so addicted have no need for their intelligence when they swear. In so doing, they are using the same vocabulary that is used by low-grade thugs and morons, criminals and prostitutes. With fine sarcasm the greatest of the poets makes his Caliban good at swearing. Caliban, you know, is a bit of a monster. He is a half-wit and a slave. But this is his boast:

"You taught me language: and my profit on't
Is, I know how to curse."

Such a boast is pathetic, even upon the lips of a half-witted monster. How doubly tragic it is on the lips of one made in the image of God. Yet there are intelligent men and women who swear as if they had been to hell for their schooling and had had the devil himself for their schoolmaster.

43

What is wrong with profanity? It is a symptom of an inner sickness. It is a stream that flows only from a poisoned and vitiated fountain. To be convinced of this, one need only realize what is indicated by a light and vulgar handling of other less sacred names than that of our Lord. There is, for instance, a coarse and dirty epithet that men at times hurl at each other that reflects upon one's mother. It is an insult that no man is willing to take. Yet not long ago a certain individual, in conversation with a minister, flippantly called himself by that filthy name. What did this indicate? It was not proof positive that his mother was a cheap and vulgar woman. But it did prove, beyond a peradventure, that she had reared a cheap and vulgar son. The only reflection upon her, of course, was being the mother of such a son. But whoever was to blame, his coarse handling of his mother's name indicated that his moral nature was honeycombed.

What would you think of a husband who would take the name of his wife in vain? Years ago, as a boy, I overheard a man who had just recently married discussing his wife with a group of other men. He spoke of her in a way that led to loud guffaws of laughter from his audience. Since then I have forgotten many things worth remembering, but this

44

ugly bit of coarseness I have never been able to forget. He posed as a teacher. But in spite of the high claim that he made for himself I have never been able to regard him with any real respect.

If we discredit those who speak in slight and flippant fashion of wife or mother, how much more should this be the case for those who flippantly take upon their lips the holy name of God. Such are profane. The word comes from two Latin words—pro, in front of, and fane, the temple. These have let their fences down. They have allowed their hearts to become a common rather than a holy place. Such a practice tends to kill that beautiful and fundamental virtue of reverence. This spells tragedy, for reverence is the very queen of the virtues. It is the doorway to every kind of knowledge. That is the reason that Jesus, when he taught us to pray, put this petition first, "Hallowed be Thy name." Reverence is the doorway into the audience chamber of the King. That door is fast shut in the face of the profane.

2. But the primary purpose of this command is not to prohibit profanity, but lying. In that distant day there were those who had, in some measure, forgotten how to tell the truth. Now these, in order to fortify their sense of obligation to truth-telling,

or, what is far more likely, in order to strengthen the confidence of their fellows in their word, got into the habit of calling God to witness to the truthfulness of what they said. But in spite of thus calling upon God, they went on with their lying. Therefore, this rule was born: "Thou shalt not take the name of the Lord thy God in vain." That is, we are not to use God's name falsely, insincerely, by calling Him to witness to a lie.

This command, then, was made necessary because men were given to lying. This lying led to swearing, and swearing to more lying. It is easy to see how this came to pass. First, men got the habit of calling God to witness to the truth of what they were saying. When, therefore, they failed to call God to witness, they did not feel quite so obligated to tell the truth. They felt bound to tell the truth only when under oath. Then, little by little, it came to pass that they did not feel bound to tell the truth, even under oath, unless they had sworn a certain kind of oath. This was the case in the days of Jesus. By that time, not only was a man's word not his bond, but this was equally true of most of his oaths. Naturally, this led to profuse and multitudinous lying. It was to correct this deadly evil that Jesus said, "Swear not at all. . . . But let your communication be, Yea, yea; Nay, nay: for whatsoever is more than these cometh of evil."

By this, I take it that Jesus does not so much mean to forbid the taking of a legal oath, as to enjoin the telling of the simple truth. There is a kinship between profane swearing and the taking of an oath. While the one is intended to make conversation more spicy, the other is intended to make one's word more strong and trustworthy. But those who have to be put under oath before they will tell the truth, will likely lie after they have taken oath. Sometime ago, for instance, a man came to my home in search of help. Though it was night, and though I had no money with me, I went with him to a neighboring drug store, cashed a check, and gave him the sum for which he asked. His appreciation knew no bounds. "I will do anything for you," he declared with abounding gratitude. "I will come in the morning and wash your car."

"All right," I answered, with not too much enthusiasm. "Come in the morning and wash my car."

"I will be there," he answered earnestly, "I will certainly be there."

Then I turned upon him with this unkind word. "Good," I said, "be sure that you come; because if you do, you will be the first man that has ever come, under similar circumstances, during the twenty-five years that I have been helping men of your kind. I do hope that you will break the record." Of course I should not have spoken so harshly. It was not only bad psychology, but cruel as well. In fact, my words pained him so that the big tears ran down his cheeks and dropped upon the pavement.

"I will surely be there," he protested earnestly. Then to make his coming an absolute certainty, he lifted his right hand, and took this solemn oath: "I hope God will strike me dead if I am not there in the morning to wash your car." And evidently that is what happened, for I have not seen him since. This commandment is a positive call to tell the simple truth.

II

THE habit of lying did not vanish with the distant day in which this commandment was written. A lie is still looked upon by many as a very present help in trouble. A wise old proverb says "Sin has a great many tools, but a lie is the handle that fits them all."

What are some of the most common forms of lying that are prevalent today?

1. First, we lie to ourselves. This we often do to excuse our moral failures. A rather bright and

flippant young man came forward at a recent service to tell me how he had broken with the church. "Why did you quit?" I asked.

"Well," he said, "it was no fault of mine." Of course, he was not telling the whole truth. The fault was his. By and by he was honest enough to say so. At times, we inflict positive wrong upon others and try to throw the responsibility for our conduct upon circumstances or upon our fellows. When David had committed adultery in the heat of passion, when he had committed murder in cold blood, he told himself that all this was no fault of his own. When he heard that Uriah was dead, he eased his outraged conscience by saying "The sword devoureth one as well as another." Thus he lied to himself.

Then we lie to ourselves when we face bullying evils or challenging opportunities and tell ourselves that there is nothing that we can do. A friend of mine took her membership out of a certain church recently. She gave as her reason that the church was cold, and that there was nothing she could do about it. A man who prided himself on being a good citizen refused to vote in a recent election, though his city is being run by well-organized crooks. This he did because he claimed there was nothing that he could do about it. But neither of these was telling the truth. There is no form of evil that we cannot in some measure weaken. There is no form of good that we cannot make the stronger. To tell ourselves otherwise is to drug ourselves by enervating lies.

2. Not only do we lie to ourselves, but we lie to our fellows. How vastly varied is this type of lying. We lie with our lips. We also lie with our lives. This we do when we play the hypocrite. This we do when we pretend that we are either better or worse than we really are. Now I do not believe that there are a great many hypocrites in the church. Certainly, their number is small in comparison with those outside the church. But wherever found, hypocrisy is a tragic and ugly evil. No other sin seems to have so aroused the indignation of Jesus. His terrific woes against the hypocrite flash like lurid lightning to this hour. This commandment, then, is against lying in all its forms, whether to ourselves or to others, whether with our lips or with our lives.

III

But why is lying forbidden?

It is forbidden because it is wrong in itself. It is humanly hurtful. By this I do not mean that there are not situations where a lie might be the lesser of two evils. But what I fear for most of us is not a too strict adherence to the truth. Our chief danger is rather in the opposite direction. What, then, I repeat, is wrong with lying? We can mention only a few of its evils.

1. Lying is anti-social. "Tell each other the truth," writes Paul, "for you are members one of another." Society depends for its stability on confidence. Confidence depends upon truth-telling. What keeps our homes together? Confidence, born of truthfulness. Not long ago I had a charming young friend who was deeply devoted to a luxury-loving girl. In order to win her, he pretended to a wealth that he did not possess. In order to keep her, once they were married, he lived beyond his means. All too soon the crash came. They are divorced to-day. Both are suffering irreparable wounds. They had builded their home upon a lie, and it toppled into ruins.

Think of the harm that lying does in the ministering to the needy. How many deserving people are cheated of help, not by the stinginess of the well-to-do, but by the lying of the unworthy! A certain minister told me this story out of his own experience. One day he had been imposed upon by an unusually large number of dead-beats. At last, exhausted, both in purse and patience, he turned a seedy chap away. Two days later they found this man's body not far from the parsonage. An autopsy showed that he had died of starvation. This minister was naturally greatly grieved. But this man was not slain by this minister, but by the liars.

How costly is lying in our international relationships! This year, it is estimated that the nations will spend at least thirteen billions of dollars in preparing for war. This tragic waste is born of a lack of confidence. This lack of confidence is born of lying. The nations have lied to each other, have regarded their treaties as "scraps of paper," till they no longer trust each other. Lying, therefore, is antisocial. No wonder God will not hold the liar guiltless.

2. But though the liar hurts others, he inflicts the deadliest injury upon himself. This is the case, in the first place, because it is not easy to live a lie. How much agony we give ourselves trying to convince our fellows that we are other than we are. Sometime ago I read of a donkey who suddenly got rich. At once he became too good to associate with his fellow donkeys. He decided to become a horse. To this end he went to the hairdresser, had his ears

trimmed and pinned down. Then he made his way into high society. He was getting on very well till he was asked to sing. As soon as he opened his mouth in song, they knew him for what he was. At first, he was greatly humiliated. But when he got back among his fellows and dared to be himself, he found a new and larger happiness.

When our boys were small, we bought them a baby phonograph. Along with it came a number of records that played Mother Goose rhymes and other worth-while poems. Among the selections was a song that I have never been able to forget.

A jolly old sow once lived in a sty,
And three little piggies had she.
She waddled about saying, "Umph, Umph, Umph,"
While the little ones said, "Wee, Wee."

"My dear little brothers," said one of the brats,
"My dear little piggies," said he,
"Let us all for the future say, 'Umph, Umph, Umph.'
It's so childish to say, 'Wee, Wee.' "

These three little piggies grew skinny and lean,
And lean they might very well be,
For, somehow, they couldn't say, "Umph, Umph, Umph,"
And they wouldn't say, "Wee, Wee, Wee."

And after a while these little pigs died,
They all died of felo-de-se,
From trying so hard to say, "Umph, Umph, Umph,"
When they only could say, "Wee, Wee."

Many people commit suicide, as did these foolish
pigs, because of the strain of trying to convince
their friends that they are other than they are.

Then lying strikes a death blow to character.
Carlyle said that if one builds a lie into a rock wall,
the wall will fall down. After the San Francisco
earthquake, Japan sent a commission to investigate
the cause of this heavy disaster. They found that
it was due more to shoddy building than to the
earthquake itself. That is, the city was builded
upon a lie, and it could not stand. The same law
holds for your life and mine. If we build upon a
lie, then when the winds blow and the floods come
and beat upon that house, it will fall, and complete
will be the wreck of it. Lying is, therefore, pro-
hibited because of the injury that it works both to
the liar and to his fellows.

IV

WHAT is involved in the keeping of this command?
It is evident that the keeping of it goes deeper than
a mere refusal to tell a lie. If that were all that

is involved, then it might be kept by a wax figure or a corpse. Therefore, this rule is a call both to live and to speak the truth.

To help us to this high end, we need a new conviction of the worth and might of the truth. A lie may win a temporary advantage, but never an abiding victory. One said of Wayne B. Wheeler that he never lost a case before the Supreme Court. To what did this writer attribute Mr. Wheeler's success? It was not so much to his great ability as to his painstaking honesty. He declared Wheeler won because every judge knew that he would tell the truth in so far as it was humanly possible. That is, he believed in the might of the truth. In so believing, he was but following in the steps of his Master. Jesus staked everything on his faith in the might of the truth. So also may we.

But to make the truth-telling a certainty, we must be true on the inside. We must be sincere. Sincerity is the fountain from which flow the springs of honesty, frankness, simplicity. This means that the best guarantee for living and speaking the truth, is to be set right at the center of one's being. We need to share the nature of Jesus that we may also share his sincerity. The sincere man will, as a rule, tell the truth spontaneously. He will tell it also as a matter of habit. But even before this fine practice becomes a habit, he will tell the truth from conviction.

Some of you will possibly remember Sam Hadley of Water Street Mission. He walked with a limp. Before his conversion, though he had never worn a uniform, he was in the habit of telling that the reason for his lameness was that he had been wounded in battle. So the day after his conversion, when a certain banker asked him about his limp, from long habit he told his same old lie. Suddenly he realized this fact, and it struck terror to his heart. He turned at once to correct it, but the banker had gone. Not to be outdone, Hadley caught the first street car, went to the banker's office, and said, "I lied to you just now." It was a humiliating experience. But he never told that lie again. Hadley had been set right on the inside. He had become sincere. This commandment, therefore, is more than a rule. It is a call to a sincerity that is born of our sharing in the Divine Nature.

REMEMBER THE SABBATH

Remember the sabbath day, to keep it holy.

EXODUS 20: 8

I

THE TEXT IS A CALL TO REMEMBER. IT IS therefore, a recognition of our proneness to forget. I know that there is a scientific sense in which we never forget anything. Every thought we think, every dream we dream, writes itself indelibly upon the tablets of the mind. But while from this scientific standpoint we never forget anything, practically we forget almost everything. Seldom a day passes that we do not bewail the fact that our own memory is so treacherous. Over and over, we hear friends complain of their own proneness to forget.

This is the case, in the first place, because we often forget of set purpose. The remembrance of certain things is annoying. Therefore, we stop thinking about them, flatly refuse to look in their direction till, little by little, we forget. Several months ago I had a letter from a man, a stranger, who was asking for help. It was an exceedingly pious letter. It fairly oozed unction. Such letters always arouse my suspicion. The writer informed me that he was too ill to come to see me, that therefore I should do well to send the sum of twelve dollars to his room at the hotel. Instead of doing so, however, I had my secretary telephone him to meet me at my office. He arrived ahead of me. When I came, he was talking to a friend of mine, a fellow minister, in the outer office. I sent him into the inner office, then inquired of my friend if he knew him. "I have seen him before," was the answer. "He borrowed some money from me once, and failed to pay me back."

Armed with this information, I went in for our interview. He told me his story, and it was a good one. But for the information I had just gained, I surely would have fallen. But instead of giving him the desired help, I asked him a few simple questions. "Do you know this minister to whom you have just been talking?" was my first question.

He thought a minute, then said, "I believe I do."

"Did you ever borrow any money from him?"

"I believe I did," was the reluctant response.

"Did you pay him back?" was my final question.

He popped his fingers in wide-eyed amazement and said, "You know, I forgot that." So some of us forget of set purpose.

Then there are those who forget unwillingly. We live at such a hectic pace that many things we fain would remember are crowded out. One day a splendid gentleman came to my study bringing an invitation to dinner for my wife and me. I was very busy; so I failed to tell Mrs. Chappell of the invitation. The result was that I never thought of it again till I was reminded by a guest who had remembered. Naturally, I was humiliated. Besides, eggs were at that time eighty cents a dozen. I forgot a wedding once, after I had attended the rehearsal. My only excuse was that unexpected company came that day and so occupied my attention that my important engagement was simply crowded out.

The truth of the matter is that there is nothing, however trivial or important, that we do not tend to forget. We forget our privileges and our opportunities. We forget our responsibilities and our obligations. We forget the vows we have made. We forget each other's names and faces. We forget our friends. Sometimes, thank God, we forget our foes. We even forget our own loved ones. We forget the things that are seen. We are especially prone to forget the things that are not seen. We even forget the God "in whose hands our breath is, and whose are all our ways."

Being thus forgetful, it is not surprising that many forget the sabbath. Some, as our borrowing friend, forget it of set purpose. They feel that it stands in their way, that it is a weight rather than wings, a barrier to shut them in rather than an open door to a finer freedom. Others forget it because life for them is so hurried and hectic. For some, it is hectic from stern necessity. They must work on that day. For others it is hectic because they are so strenuously in pursuit either of gold or of pleasure. But be the causes what they may, this day is for many a forgotten day. Therefore we need this urgent call: "Remember the sabbath day, to keep it holy."

II

WHAT are we to remember about the sabbath?

1. We ought to remember that the sabbath is God's gift to man, that it was given, not for the benefit of God, but for the benefit of ourselves. It fits into human need. In this it is like every other of these rules. Not one of them is for God's benefit; all are for ours. We realize, of course, that our sabbath is not the same as that observed by the Jews. Theirs was the seventh day of the week, while ours is the first. The reason we observe the first day instead of the seventh is based on no positive command. One will search the Scriptures in vain for authority for changing from the seventh day to the first. The early Christians began to worship on the first day of the week because Jesus rose from the dead on that day. By and by, this day of worship was made also a day of rest, a legal holiday. This took place in the year 321.

Our Christian sabbath, therefore, is not a matter of positive command. It is a gift of the church. The church not only gave us our sabbath; it also gave us our New Testament. It gave us the new world that was born of the spread of the Kingdom of God. We are, therefore, to think of our Christian sabbath as a day set apart under the leadership of the Spirit. Of course the vital matter is not what day we observe, but that we observe one day in seven. This one day, which is for us the Christian Sunday, is God's gift, that we are to receive with thanksgiving.

Now since Sunday is a gift, we can receive it or reject it. The fact that some friend offers you a gift does not mean that you are compelled to accept it. I knew a man once who offered a girl an engagement ring, but she refused it. I knew a church to offer its pastor a car as a gift, but, for some reason, he refused to accept it. I knew a father to offer his son an opportunity for an education, but the son flippantly turned the offer down. The truth is that nobody can give us what we are not willing to receive. This is true not only of our fellows; it is true of God as well. He cannot even give us life eternal unless we are willing to receive it. No more can he give us the sabbath.

When, therefore, God offers this gift, there are some that turn from it, counting it a hindrance rather than a help. This is the case with that large group that treats Sunday just as any other day. We all know some of these broad-minded chaps. "Every day ought to be holy," they tell us flippantly. "Sunday means no more to me than Monday." But to treat Sunday in this fashion is to throw it away. "The sabbath," said Jesus, "was made for man."

Unless that statement is plain nonsense, Jesus meant that the sabbath was to be used in a fashion a bit different from other days. It was to be unique. To refuse to treat it so is to reject this precious gift.

Then there are those who accept the gift only to misuse it. These are divided roughly into two groups. First, there are those who misuse the sabbath by making it a day of repression rather than expression. Jesus found that the Pharisees had fallen into this error. They had changed the sabbath from a day of joy to a day of gloom. This they had done by hedging it about by hundreds of rigid rules. There were more than fifteen hundred ways in which a man might break the sabbath. They were so numerous, in fact, that it took a great scholar to know them all.

For instance, one could not kindle a fire on the sabbath. If a man's ox fell into a ditch on the sabbath, he might pull him out; but if the man himself fell in, he had to stay there. If he should take a sup of vinegar for food, that was permissible; but if he should take a sup in order to help his aching tooth, he had broken the sabbath. If he was bitten by a flea, he was compelled to permit the little pest to keep on his annoying work. To undertake to catch it was to be guilty of the sin of hunting. In fact, one saint suggested that the proper way to observe the sabbath was to lie in exactly the same position for twenty-four hours. In later years the Puritans fell somewhat into the same error. There is a story of a certain sea captain who returned to his home in Massachusetts after an absence of two years. His wife met him at the gate, and he kissed her. But it was not lawful to kiss one's wife on the sabbath. Therefore, this wicked captain was put in the stocks for his lack of reverence for this holy day. It was this attitude toward the sabbath that made it for many a day of ugliness and horror.

It was against such use of this day of privilege that Jesus blazed with hot indignation. He reminded these Pharisees that they were trying to fit man into the sabbath, thus forgetting that man was not made for the sabbath, but that the sabbath was made for man. With Jesus, always, the supreme values were human values. Man is not made for the state, but the state is made for man. Jesus was and is against any use of the sabbath that fails to make human need of supreme importance. Yet there have been those who have made Sunday a blue day by hedging it about by rigid rules.

But if the Sunday of our fathers was blue, ours seems to be a bit scarlet. As I suggested in my sermon, "The Forgotten Day," Sunday is now for many the most hectic day of the week. It is the day in which those whose business it is to amuse us have to work the hardest. It is day when we have some of our biggest athletic contests. It is the day when many, even of our church people, give their most elaborate parties. It is the day for our biggest picnics. It is the day on which we try to get enough exercise to last us an entire week, when we try to get enough sunburn to take a full six days to heal. It is the day when the largest crowds flock to our theaters. It is the day when our roads are most congested by traffic. It is the day that we send the greatest number of wounded to our hospitals. It is the day on which we send the largest number of slaughtered to our morgues. Surely the day is no longer blue, but scarlet.

As Christian people we need to realize that this change of attitude toward Sunday has not come about through reasoned convictions on the part of religious people. We have taken our cue from the world rather than the world from us. We have not so much thought our way to our new position as drifted into it under the spell of the world. I can remember when the influence of the church was sufficiently strong to secure Sunday as a holy day for many. I can remember, for instance, when decent worldly people would not attend Sunday shows. Actors themselves used to say that the most stupid, dull, moronic crowds to which they ever showed were the Sunday evening crowds. But this Sunday night, if all the church members that are in the theaters of this city were to come into our services, every church would be crowded to the doors.

Then we need to realize, further, that those who have led us into our new use of Sunday have not been actuated by the highest possible motives. No more have we in our following, sheeplike, after them. Why have so many, both within and without the church, come to misuse Sunday? They have sacrificed this day upon the altar of the twin gods, pleasure and profit. Some misuse Sunday in an effort, that is generally futile, to have a good time. Others use it in order to make money out of it. Thus the motives that are robbing us of Sunday are the same that lie back of about all the evils that vex us. Take the liquor problem, for instance. Who destroyed Prohibition? Two groups, those who were bent on the pleasure of drinking liquor and those who were bent on making money out of it. Rid us of these two groups and liquor will be no more a problem than sassafras tea.

"So what?" is the question of the modern man. "Why should we not use Sunday as a holiday and as a holiday only, if we so desire?" It is a fair question. My answer is this: it is not that the engaging in all these pastimes is necessarily bad in itself. To make only a holiday of Sunday is certainly better than forgetting it altogether. But though this is one use, it is not the only one, nor the highest. This is the case because man is more than an animal. He is even more than a highly intelligent animal. He is an immortal soul. Sunday is intended to minister to the needs of the whole man, to those that are physical and temporal, and also to those that are spiritual and eternal. Therefore, to make of Sunday a holiday only is to misuse it.

Then such a practice is wrong because no man lives to himself. If I persist in misusing Sunday I thereby rob someone else. My buying gasoline on Sunday compels somebody to sell it. My baseball game requires strenuous toil on the part of at least eighteen others. Even my innocent golf may keep some caddy from the church services or the Sunday school. The sabbath was made for man, the whole man, and for all men. Therefore, I have no right to use it in such a fashion as to rob either myself or others of its highest usefulness. To do so is to accept this precious gift only to misuse it. But we need neither reject nor misuse Sunday. We may accept it and thus be enriched by it.

III

How, then, are we to use Sunday?

1. It is to be a day of rest. Of course, rest implies work. Man was intended to be a worker. Work was not sent upon us as a curse, but as one of life's greatest blessings. A curse that is a curse indeed is idleness—whether it is voluntary or enforced. Every man ought to have to work. Every man has a right to work. There is no surer sign of a diseased social order than the fact that some are idle because they do not have to work, while others are idle because, though eager to work, they have no opportunity.

But while work is an unmeasured blessing, man is not to work all the time. He needs one day in seven upon which to rest. This is the case whether he works with hand or brain. Man can do more in six days than he can in seven. To disregard this fact is to lower vitality and efficiency. It is to bring on frayed nerves, broken bodies, and premature death. A friend told of seeing two groups of donkeys at a certain mountain resort. These donkeys were used to take sightseers to the top of a lofty mountain. "One group," he declared, "looked well kept, but the other was lean and weary, with no seeming interest in life." Why the difference? One man sent his donkeys up the mountain seven days a week; the other refused to work his more than six days. The difference in their appearance indicated that even a donkey knows that one day in seven should be used as a day of rest.

This day of rest was intended especially to protect those whose time was not their own. It gave even the slaves a chance. I can remember hearing the Negroes sing a song that came up out of their own experiences of sabbath rest and sabbath joy. The refrain of that song was this: "Every day will be Sunday by-and-by." To them, Sunday was a day when the heavy load was loosed from their shoulders, when they could have a little time to knit up "the ravelled sleeve of care." It was a day so sweet and restful that when they thought of heaven, they thought of it as a place where this joyful and restful day would last forever. Therefore, they sang in their plaintive fashion, "Every day will be Sunday by-and-by."

2. It is to be a day that offers an opportunity for

worship. Now just as universal as our need for rest, is our need for worship. The Christian Sunday began as a day of worship. To worship aright, we need a bit of time, a bit of leisure. "Be still and know that I am God." Life is too hectic for most of us. We do not have time to appreciate the beauty in the world of nature. What Wordsworth said of his day would be far more true of the pushful day in which our lot is cast:

> "The world is too much with us; late and soon,
> Getting and spending, we lay waste our powers;
> Little we see in nature that is ours."

If our hurry has so robbed us that we have little in nature that is ours, we have, I fear, still less in God. It is through worship that we come into the realization of those unseen values that abide. It is as we worship that our stained lives are made clean. It is as we worship that we are recommissioned and rededicated to high aims and purposes. It was while the disciples were worshiping that Jesus said, "As the Father hath sent me, even so send I you." It was as they were worshiping that they were empowered for their task. "He breathed on them, and saith unto them, receive ye the Holy Spirit." To worship is to grow spiritually strong. "Even the youth shall faint and be weary, and the young man shall utterly fall! But they that wait upon the Lord, shall renew their strength." Jesus knew the value of worship, hence we read that he went into the synagogue on the Sabbath, as his custom was.

The highest use of Sunday, then, and far the most rewarding, is to make it a day of worship and rest. Worship and rest, these two go together. When we cease to worship, the pull of the world is likely to rob us of our day of rest. When we cease to rest, we are likely also to cease to worship. Everybody, then, needs this holy day. We simply cannot manage life aright without it. We need it for ourselves. We need it because it gives us our best opportunity to teach religion. When we forget this day, we are on the way to forgetting God. When we forget God, we turn our backs on life and lose our souls. Therefore, not as an end, but as a means to the high end of being and doing our best, we ought to remember the sabbath to keep it holy.

V

HONOR YOUR PARENTS

*Honor thy father and thy mother:
that thy days may be long upon the
land which the Lord thy God giveth
thee.*

EXODUS 20: 12

I

HERE IS A WORD THAT CALLS FOR AN ATTITUDE of respect, reverence, and obedience on the part of children toward their parents. How shockingly old-fashioned it sounds to our modern ears! Some of us hear it with a superior smile, or even with positive antagonism. This is not surprising, since it speaks to us out of a long gone past. The situation that gave it birth was far different from ours. It was born of the needs of a primitive people from whom we are separated by seas and continents and centuries. At that distant day, the father's will was supreme. His child was his property. In our day, thanks to our Lord, the child has taken its place in the center.

Then we tend to look askance at this ancient rule because it calls for the recognition of authority. We of today are rather impatient of authority of any kind. Our modern version of this rule is not, "Children, obey your parents in the Lord: for this is right," as Paul states it. It is rather, "Parents, obey your children, for you can't afford to be bothered." There is even a very wise youth now and then who is big and broad-minded enough to tell his parents frankly and to their faces that he did not ask to be born. Since, therefore, life has been wished on him without his consent he has the right to shrug all responsibility off his shoulders.

Of course, he did not ask to be born. I am quite sure, further, that his parents would never have asked for him to have been if they had known that he was going to be a perpetual infant. Whoever makes a statement of this kind gives positive proof that he has never even begun to grow up. He is a moral runt, a pathetic spiritual dwarf. It is said that a certain father was reading the evening lesson for family prayer just after his son had come home in disgrace from his fifth school. The lesson related to the golden calf. "I cast my gold into the fire, and behold there came forth this calf," he read, and added, as he looked meaningly at his son, "The only word I need to change to fit my case is to put schools instead of fire."

Then some resent this rule because they believe that it puts emphasis upon the debt that children owe to parents rather than upon the debt that parents owe to children. But this is not the case at all. Therefore, instead of stirring our antagonism, this rule ought to win our hearty approval. "Honor thy father and thy mother." What is the purpose of this rule? To the minds of many it is seeking the well-being and happiness of fathers and mothers. It is seeking to guarantee to them the joy that comes from obedient children. It is trying to spare them the pain and anguish of being dishonored and neglected. Its purpose is to save parents the tragedy of knowing "how sharper than a serpent's tooth it is to have a thankless child."

But this is not the primary purpose of the rule at all. While loyalty to it would spare parents endless pain and heartache, while obedience to it would bring them unmeasured joy, its real purpose is not to safeguard parents, but to safeguard youth. It does not look toward the past, but toward the future. This is evident when we notice the ones who are to profit through obedience to it. This rule has a promise attached to it, Paul reminds us. But this promise is not to parents, but to children. "Children, obey your parents in the Lord: for this is right . . . that it may be well with thee, and thou mayest live long on the earth."

II

"Honor thy father and thy mother." But why? is the natural and legitimate answer. "Because," the Apostle replies, "such a course is right." It is right in the nature of things. It is right because it is humanly helpful. "How much is three times three?" I ask. "Nine," is your answer. "Right!" is my response. There is the same fundamental rightness in this rule. But if this is true, wherein is it true?

1. It is right for children to honor their parents, in the first place, because their parents know more than they. This rule assumes superior knowledge on the part of parents. It assumes that a mother will know more at thirty than her daughter will know at three. It assumes that a father will know more at forty than his son at four. Of course, your case may be an exception. But this is the bold

assumption on which this command rests. It dares to assume that fathers and mothers learn something by the very process of living. They learn, perchance, that fire burns, that the law of gravitation always operates. They learn something of the roads that lead into the depths, and of those that lead into the heights. They learn something of material values. They are supposed also to learn something of those values that are spiritual and abiding. This rule declares, further, that it is the child's right to share in the treasures of this accumulated knowledge.

In young and tender years the normal child is quite ready to believe in the superior wisdom of his parents, and to profit by it. But some reach a period, quite early in life, when they become superior. "You know quite a bit," a friend of mine said to a group of young girl graduates. Their evident approval seemed to say, "Quite right. You are speaking even more wisely than you realize." "But you do not intend to quit learning," he continued. "You do not expect to become victims of arrested development. You expect to know far more twenty-five years from now than you know today." At once they nodded their heads in eager approval.

"Since that is the case," this wise teacher continued, "it is well for you to remember that your mothers have had just about that much start of you. Therefore, when you get home you might listen to them a bit." Generally speaking, this is a very sane word. I know there may be exceptions. You may be very wise, and your parents very foolish. You may be very brilliant, and they very dull. But bear in mind that even a tortoise beat a fleet-footed hare in a race one time. This he did, not because he was swifter than the hare, but because he got an earlier start. Since the child is quite a few years behind his parents, it might be for his good to honor and obey them.

This rule not only assumes the superior knowledge of parents, but it assumes further that the right to rule belongs to those who know rather than to those who do not. In the book of Genesis, for instance, God is represented as saying to man, "Have dominion." That is, man is to bring his environment and all lower orders of life into subjection. But how is he to do this, and by what right? How has he done it increasingly through the centuries? It has not been by mere force. In physical strength there are many animals that are his superior. In a hand-to-hand combat the lion could whip him any day. The deer could outrun him. Any sort of bird could outfly him. The elephant could shout louder than he.

Yet today this physically weak creature can outrun the antelope, outswim the fish, whip the lion, shout louder than the elephant, and outfly the eagle. This is the case not because he has grown into a physical monstrosity. His triumphs are natural results of his superior knowledge!

2. Now, there are times when children are not willing to share the parents' knowledge. Here is when the need for discipline arises. For instance, when your small boy makes up his mind to play with your razor instead of his toy dog, then what? When he insists upon drinking Lysol instead of sweet milk, upon eating mud instead of spinach, what about it? When he decides that he does not believe in education, and therefore refuses to go to school, what course do you pursue? Well, you talk it over with him and explain the wisdom and rightness of your position. If he fails to listen, then you resort to other means. You may even try a bit of kindly compulsion. It would be at once criminal and silly to do otherwise. That is, you will not allow a child unlimited choice either as to food, playthings, or school, knowing that he has not sufficient data upon which to go.

The necessity for wise and kindly discipline in another realm is equally needful. It has become the fashion among certain parents to refuse to give their children any religious training, leaving them to reach their own conclusions. This is just as deadly in the realm of the spiritual as it would be in the realm of the physical. A bit of wholesome constraint toward religion is vastly helpful, in spite of that mythical character who never goes to church today because he was forced to go when he was a boy. He may exist, but he is about as rare as those who cannot read because they were forced to attend school in boyhood. Those who are carrying on the work of the church today are those who, either willingly or unwillingly, attended as boys and girls. I believe, therefore, in the right kind of discipline for the forming of right habits.

Then discipline is good because everybody needs to learn to obey. Even Jesus had to learn obedience through the things that he suffered. Every child needs to learn obedience because there is no happiness without it. One can put it down as a fundamental fact that no child is ever happy whose will is never crossed. I am thinking now of a bright and wretched little savage who could be happy and civilized if his parents were only wise enough to control him. But they take the all-too-common view that he is too wonderful to curb, that to exercise any authority over him would take a bit of the blue out of his sky. Therefore, they let him run wild. As a consequence his face is usually a picture of snarling discontent. He demands to be amused every hour of his waking existence. He has not the slightest initiative in amusing himself. Therefore, instead of being a normal and happy child, he is abnormal and unhappy.

Not only is he restless and wretched in himself, but he increases his natural peevishness and discontent by making himself a holy terror to those about him. Boys and girls of his own age do not like to play with him because he knows nothing of the give and take of the game; he must take all the time. His father and mother still love him, strange as it may seem, but they are about all. His presence to the other members of the family is about as soothing as the itch, and about as exhilarating as a dust storm. Of course the parents are far more to blame than the child; but in thus failing to teach him discipline they are cheating not only him, but others as well.

The saddest part of this story is likely yet to be told. Failing to learn discipline in the home, he is likely to suffer for it, and to make others suffer for it, the deeper he gets into life. Such a child finds every relationship more difficult than if he had learned obedience. His inward anarchy will tend to make him an anarchist in every relationship of life. Take marriage, for instance. He has learned that if he will stomp his foot hard enough, scream loud enough, quarrel long enough, he can always have his way. What will happen if he meets a girl brought up in the same kind of home? That will likely take place which occurs when an irresistible force hits an unmovable body; there will be a catastrophe. This is the secret of many wrecked marriages today.

This also accounts for the failure of many to submit to the discipline of the state. The biggest business in America today is the crime business. From whence do these criminals come? They come out of our homes. As a rule, they come out of homes where wholesome discipline was not known. They find it easy to break the laws of the land because they have never known what it is to submit to any law. Now, I am not arguing for a brutal type of discipline. I am only pleading that you give your child a chance. I am asking you, for love's sake, to give your child the kind of discipline that will fit him for life. You are to do this, even though it may be painful for both of you. If your boy should break his leg, you would have it set, even though it might be painful. You would not, to save him from temporary agony, allow him to grow up a cripple. Nor should you, to save him from the pain of discipline, allow him to grow up a moral cripple.

3. Finally, it is a privilege for children to obey their parents because by so doing they find it easier and more natural to obey their heavenly Father. This is the reason that obedience to this rule has the promise of both well-being and of length of days. That is, those who obey live more richly, other things being equal, than those who do not. This they do, not as a reward, but as a consequence. This they do because those who learn to play the game of life according to the rules play it better and stay in the game longer. The truth of this has been demonstrated times without number. For this reason, every child ought to have the privilege of obedience.

III

"Honor thy father and thy mother." How is obedience to this command to be brought about?

Let it be said at once that the weightier part of responsibility rests upon the shoulders of the parents. Fathers and mothers can conduct themselves in such a fashion that for their children to honor them would be either a tragedy or an utter impossibility. Children naturally look up to their parents. Suppose these are worthless and unworthy, then what? The more they honor such parents, the worse it will be for them. This is the case because we tend to become like those we honor. The child that worships an image of clay is likely to get dust and dirt, not upon its knees only, but upon its soul as well.

Then there are times when children cannot honor parents because they know them for what they are. And mark me! they usually do. Parents do not often deceive children. If you are a sham and a fraud, beware of the clear eyes of your boys and girls. In talking to a father some time ago, I urged upon him the importance of right living for the sake of his children. "I do not let them know what I do," he replied. But they knew far more than he thought. When a little later he became a Christian, his small boy said with great pride, "We have got good times in our house now, since Daddy got religion." God pity us, when we make it impossible for our children to honor us, or to do so only at their peril.

But there is a way to insure respect and honor on the part of our children. The first step in this direction, as hinted above, is the right exercise of parental authority. We should never get the idea that children will love and honor a parent the less because he controls them. If he deals fairly with them, if he is reasonable and just and loving, if he avoids nagging, if he takes time to give them himself, they will respond. Not only so, but they will respect him far more for controlling them than for not doing so. Listen to mature men and women of today as they speak of their own parents. Those who speak with reverence and tenderness and honor are, as a rule, those who had parents that controlled them in their young and tender years.

Then we can compel their respect and honor by being the kind of man or woman that we ought to be. What are the qualities in your own father and mother that have held your honor and respect through the years? What was it about them that to this day brings your soul to its knees? It was not the beauty of your mother, though she may have been a beautiful woman. It was not the superb intelligence of your father, though he was doubtless intelligent. That, above all else, which wins and holds respect and reverence is sincerity, unselfishness, in short, genuine goodness. We cannot resist those, if we have any worth at all, who have lovingly lifted us upon their toil-worn hands that we might see more than they have seen, and be more than they have been.

But if the heavier part of this obligation rests upon the parents, that does not mean that the children are exempt. The author of this rule believes that there is a debt that children owe to parents. This is not a popular position, but it is a true one. This I say, realizing that many parents are not worthy. I know that not every woman who gives birth to a child is a real mother. Not every man who shares with some woman and with God in the creation of a child is a real father. But, in spite of this fact, the chances are that your parents, commonplace as they may be, are worthy of a bit of honor and respect on your part. If you decide at least to give them the advantage of the doubt, you will gladden them, and perhaps save yourself some bitter regrets.

Since obedience involves mutual obligation, how wise it would be for parents and children to put themselves each in the place of the other. First, we fathers and mothers ought to put ourselves in the place of our children. That should be comparatively easy for us, since we were once young. For you boys and girls to put yourselves in our place

85

would naturally be more difficult, since you have never been our age. But, if you could have imagination enough and heart enough to do it, it would be vastly rewarding, both for ourselves and for you. Remember this, at least, that the things that are worrying us now will be worrying you twenty-five years from now. Bear in mind also, that, though we may have lost step, though our commands seem at times harsh and silly, we love you better than anybody else. If you respond to this love, we believe you will be the better for it in the here and now. Then, one day you may come to our graves and find something blooming there sweeter than spring violets and fairer than the lilies of the valley. It will be the memory of a father and mother who could bless you in their homegoing. Therefore, "Honor thy father and thy mother."

VI

REVERENCE HUMAN LIFE

Thou shalt not kill.

EXODUS 20: 13

W HAT A STRANGE TEXT TO USE IN ADDRESSING
a group of professing Christians! To warn
you not to kill seems about as futile and useless as
a rain at sea. The temptation to take the life of
another has never been a major temptation with
many of you. I doubt if we have as many as a
half-dozen gangsters or professional gunmen in this
audience. But, in spite of this fact, this ancient
law does have something to say to us. There is
really more here than meets the eye.

I

WHAT is forbidden by this rule?

1. We are forbidden to take life directly, as did
Cain when he slew his brother. We are also for-

bidden to kill by proxy as did David when he murdered Uriah. This law recognizes the sacredness of life; it recognizes the fact that life is God's gift. We have power to take it, but we have no power to restore it. To kill, therefore, is a wrong that once done, it cannot be undone. There is a fatal finality about it. When Othello had made up his mind to kill the woman that he loved, it was the thought of this finality that haunted him. Once done, it could never be undone.

"Put out the light,—and then put out the light—
 If I quench thee, thou flaming minister,
 I can again thy former light restore,
 Should I repent me;—but, once put out thy light,
 Thou cunning'st pattern of excelling nature,
 I know not where is that Promethean heat,
 That can thy light relume."

2. Then this law forbids suicide. "You are not your own," says Paul; "you are bought with a price." Your life belongs to God; it belongs also to your fellows. To fling it away is wrong. It is, as a rule, to play the coward. Many a man, having made a mess of life through his own folly, finds himself face to face with difficulties that he has not the gallantry to meet. He, therefore, proceeds to dodge out of life by suicide, thus leaving the bur-

dens that he should have carried to be borne by others. Most of us recognize suicide on the part of the sane as essentially wrong.

Not only is it wrong for us to kill ourselves directly by a gun or by poison; it is also wrong to kill ourselves by degrees, by some form of dissipation. The man who digs his grave with his teeth is guilty before God and his fellows. To indulge in any pleasure at the price of premature death is wrong, however innocent that pleasure may seem. Some time ago a friend of mine said to me as he lighted a cigarette, "I have a tobacco heart. My doctor has told me that if I do not quit smoking it is going to kill me. I did quit for a while, but I missed it so much that I made up my mind that I would rather die sooner than to deny myself the pleasure of smoking." In my opinion, that man, and every man who does day by day that which he believes will shorten his life, is, in some measure, guilty before God of the breaking of this commandment.

3. But the violation of this law that brings most of us under condemnation is of a nature that will never brand us as in any sense criminal. It is easy to break this law without ever getting ourselves arrested. We may break it and never see the inside of a jail. We may certainly break it and run no risk

of the gallows or of the electric chair. It is altogether possible for us to have our brother's blood upon our hands, and yet never be sufficiently conscious of it to cry with Lady Macbeth, "Out, damned spot! out, I say!"

For instance, this rule forbids our exposing either ourselves or others to needless physical risks. Of course, it is right, and often our sacred duty, to venture our lives in a worthy cause. We honor those who, through the years, have not counted their lives as dear unto themselves that they might bring help and enrichment to others. We honor those who have toiled for this end in the realm of the spiritual. We also honor those who, like Walter Reed in his battle with yellow fever, have dared ghastly death in order to destroy some deadly disease. There is no price too great to pay in order to fulfil our mission of service to our fellows.

But so many of our risks are at once silly and sinful. Day after day, in our city, both men and women are hailed before our courts for reckless driving while in a state of intoxication. Liquor has this devilish effect: it dulls our finer faculties, and arouses our baser ones. It stupefies Dr. Jekyl and stimulates Mr. Hyde. The modest girl becomes less modest after a few cocktails. The timid man becomes more bold. The partially intoxicated driver is emboldened to take risks that he would not otherwise take. But while liquor increases his daring, it diminishes his capacity to handle both himself and his machine. Liquor slows our reactions. We cannot crook a finger, we cannot bat an eye, we cannot throw on the brakes as quickly under the influence of liquor as when sober. The man, therefore, who drives a car while even slightly under the influence of drink is a potential killer. That is also true of those who are intoxicated by sheer love of speed. We kill more each year than were killed in the World War because we thus expose ourselves and others to needless physical risks.

This rule calls also for the safest possible working conditions. The employer has no right to expose his employee to needless risks. It calls for sanitary housing. No landlord has the right to expose the one who rents his property to needless risks. This law calls for a chance to work for a living wage. The individual or the social order that helps to rob another of bread so that his vitality is so lowered as to make him an easy prey of disease is guilty of the violation of this law. No man, I repeat, has a right to expose his brother to a needless physical risk.

This rule also forbids the exposing ourselves or

others to needless moral risks. It recognizes the fact that a man must have not only something to live on, but something to live for. We can kill our brother as surely by robbing him of his incentives to live as by the use of a gun. Without something to live for he may fling out of life by his own hand, or he may die of sheer loss of interest. I am thinking now of a lovely little girl who belonged to my church in the city of Memphis. Love came to her with the dawn of womanhood, and she gave her all to a man who promised to make her happy. But that man trailed their orange blossoms through the mud. By and by he forsook her altogether and went away with another woman. The news came a few days ago that this girl had died by her own hand. She was wrong in taking that course, I know. But the supreme load of her guilt rests, not upon herself, but upon the man that robbed her of that which made life for her worth the living.

The truth is that we can kill in the most tragic fashion without any blood-letting at all. We can kill by our cruelty, by our ingratitude, by our neglect. We can kill by exposing our weaker brother to needless temptation. "I killed him!" an old schoolmate of mine said of a mutual friend of ours, some years ago. "I led him into dissipation. I was strong enough to take it; he was not. I killed him. His blood is on my hands."

Did you read that pathetic letter that appeared in our papers last week? It was written by one who called herself "The Little Girl in Gray." She wrote it just before she swallowed the fatal draught that took her life. "Nobody is to blame for what I now do," she wrote, "except myself and my father." She did not accuse her father of giving her the poison. She accused him of a wrong that made this seem the only way out. Therefore, she took her plunge into the unknown with this grim word upon her lips: "Good-bye, Dad; I'll see you in hell." This rule forbids our exposing another to needless moral risks.

Then I believe this rule has something to say to those whose business it is to enforce the law. It also has something to say to our sluggish public conscience that is so indifferent about law-enforcement. Chief Justice Taft said years ago that the enforcement of our criminal law constituted a national disgrace. Surely, he was right. We surpass in our blood-letting any other nation in the world. We kill approximately 12,000 every year. An ordinary American city has more homicides per year than England, Ireland, Scotland, and Wales. The vast

93

majority of these crimes go unpunished. Public opinion is too lax. Too often we have criminal lawyers who are criminal in the strictest sense of the word. In Gilbert Parkers' *The Right Way,* Steele, a brilliant lawyer, secures a favorable verdict for his client who is charged with murder. Freed from the menace of death, he hurries to the lawyer to thank him. "Get away," said Steele, with loathing, "you are as guilty as hell." But if the client was guilty, and known to be so, so was his defender. To let a dangerous criminal loose on the public is a crime, whether it is done by a lawyer, or a jury, a governor, or a parole board.

Finally, I believe that this commandment forbids war. I am not forgetting that this was not its orginal purpose. The Jews were a warlike people. They believed that Jehovah was a god of war. I am remembering also that the more correct translation of this rule is not, "Thou shalt not kill," but, "Thou shalt do no murder." Nor am I claiming that every man that kills in war is a murderer. All through history there have been men of outstanding saintliness who have engaged in the bloody brutalities of war.

But this does not mean that war is right for us. There were those that burned helpless women as witches who felt no sense of guilt. But we have come upon better days. We have more light than our fathers had. We have, therefore, come to face the fact that war is the supreme killer of all history. Once it killed only the fighter; today, it kills combatants, and noncombatants as well. It lays its hands not only upon the wielder of the sword, but upon helpless women and children. Realizing this, an increasing number of us feel that we could no more kill men in the mass than we could kill in single combat. Therefore, to engage in war would be for us a violation of this command.

II

BUT this ancient rule not only forbids actual killing, but also those attitudes and passions that lead to the taking of life. Jesus not only forbids the striking of the fatal blow, he forbids the passion that prompts the blow. "Ye have heard that it was said by them of old time, Thou shalt not kill. . . . But I say unto you, that whosoever is angry with his brother without cause shall be in danger," etc. To the mind of Jesus selfish anger is wrong. It is wrong because such anger is incipient murder. If a man is angry with another, the difference between

95

him and the one who kills is in degree rather than in kind.

This does not mean, of course, that all anger is wrong. Jesus sometimes flamed with anger. There are times when anger is not only permissible, but a solemn duty. There is an anger that is in the highest sense right. Such was the anger of Jesus. This was the case not because of who he was; it was the case because his anger was born, not of selfishness, as ours usually is, but of unselfishness. Then his anger was right, in the second place, because it did not give him a passion to injure those against whom he was angry, but only to help and to save them. An anger born of love and that seeks to save, is right. But our kind of anger is usually dangerous, and may become deadly.

2. This commandment not only forbids anger, but that which is the outgrowth of cherished anger, and that is hate. One danger of anger is that it tends to harden into hate. That is the reason Paul says, "Let not the sun go down on your wrath." Shun hate because the hater is a potential killer. The Apostle of love tells us that he that hateth his brother is a murderer. Therefore avoid hate as you would avoid the spilling of blood.

3. Finally this rule forbids another attitude that is

deadly, and that is indifference. If anger and hate
have slain their thousands, crass indifference has
slain its tens of thousands. This is perhaps the
deadliest sin, both of those within the church and
without it. There are some of us that dare not look
at our world; we dare not face our own homes, our
own city, because of the disturbing sights we may
see. And we are not willing to be disturbed. Jesus
uttered not a few parables of solemn warning while
he was among us. But not one of these was against
aggressive killers. He did not warn us against becoming gunmen and gangsters. He warned us rather
against that smug indifference that can pass by a
wounded brother and leave him to die. To move
in the midst of the desperately needy, the sorely
wounded, and be indifferent, is to be guilty of a
brother's blood.

III

How are we to keep this command?

Of course, it is not enough that we refrain from
doing our brother actual bodily harm. A corpse or a
wax figure could be obedient after that fashion.
We can obey this rule in the Christian sense, not by
merely driving out anger, hate, and indifference, but
by bringing in their opposites. We can obey this

97

rule only by possessing a good will toward our fellows that is active, aggressive, and sacrificial. To do this we must have something of the high sense of human worth possessed by our Lord. According to Jesus, the one object of supreme worth in this world was man. Over and over he sought to burn that conviction into our hearts. One day he held a pair of balances in his hand. Into one pan of those balances he put the whole world. Into the other he put man, not a certain type of man, just any man. And the world flew up as if it were as light as a bit of thistledown. "What will it profit a man if he gain the whole world and lose himself?" We need to have Jesus' sense of the supreme worth of human personality.

Possessed by this, we shall give ourselves to the task of fighting all that wars against man, and to the establishing of all that seeks to enrich his life. There is a story of a certain queen named Lygia, who was captured in the north country, in the early days of Christianity, and brought to Rome. With her came also her servant Ursus, a great giant of a man, who was bound to her by the deepest loyalty. Soon after their arrival, they were both converted to this new religion of love. Here, too, a Roman patrician met Lygia and loved her with such passionate devotion that he was won to her faith. Then came those terrible days of persecution under Nero, when the cry arose with cruel savagery, "The Christians to the lions!" Among those destined for slaughter were Lygia and her faithful servant, Ursus.

The hour for execution has struck. Thousands are gathered together in the arena to see the show. There is a blare of trumpets, a grating is slipped back, and into the arena walks this splendid giant. Rome has never seen his like before. He makes his way to the center of the arena and bows in prayer. There are hisses from the spectators. They are tired of seeing men die like sheep. They want to see these great muscles brought into play. But they soon lapse into silence, for they know not what may happen when this giant meets death eye to eye. There is another blare of trumpets. Then there dashes into the arena a great, wild bull, on whose horns is bound the nude form of a woman. The praying giant opens his eyes and sees that this woman is his queen. He springs to his feet, as if touched by living fire, dashes down the arena, seizes the wild beast by the horns, and stops him in his tracks. The giant's feet sink slowly into the sand. His head almost disappears between his shoulders. The feet of the bull also sink into the sand, while his body is bent like a drawn bow. They are so still that the bewildered spectators feel that they are gazing upon some enormous statue.

But in that seeming repose there is the determined struggle of two contending forces. Which will fall first? That is a question that to those people means, for the moment, more than the destiny of their empire. Then slowly, almost imperceptibly at first, the head of the beast begins to turn in the hands of the man. His tongue lolls from his shaggy jaws. Then those sitting close enough hear the breaking of bones, and the great beast turns upon his side, his neck twisted in death. The giant, with nimble fingers, frees his queen, lifts her, and puts her into the arms of the man who loves her. This has been the work of Christianity through the centuries. But the task is not yet finished. Upon the horns of the wild beast of anger and hate, greed and war, much of our humanity still is bound. Therefore, in obedience to this command we are to go forth against all that would rob the weakest of our fellows of a place at the feast of the fulness of life.

VII

KEEP CLEAN

Thou shalt not commit adultery.

EXODUS 20: 14

SOME OF THE RULES THAT WE HAVE STUDIED SO far have, no doubt, seemed rather dusty and out of date. But such is not the case with the one that we are now to consider. It speaks home to our needs as if written in a peculiar sense for ourselves. Our day has witnessed a tremendous moral let-down. This let-down has been nowhere more pronounced than in our change of attitude toward this commandment. Many are skeptical about it, and others are in more or less open rebellion against it. So much is this the case that it is my opinion that relationships between the sexes have been more lax since the World War than in any other period in our history.

Therefore, this rule speaks home to us with peculiar timeliness and urgency.

I

WHAT do we mean by adultery?

1. Let it be said at once that we are considering this word as defined by the New Testament rather than by the Old. Its first and simplest meaning is unfaithfulness in the marriage relationship on the part of either the husband or the wife. Jesus gave his conception of marriage in the following words: "For this cause shall a man leave father and mother, and shall cleave to his wife: and they twain shall be one flesh. Wherefore they are no more twain, but one flesh. What therefore God hath joined together, let not man put asunder."

Here Jesus makes four affirmations concerning marriage that seem to me to be fundamental: (1) Marriage is a divine institution. It is a part of God's plan for us, and therefore belongs to the eternal fitness of things. (2) It is the highest human relationship. It takes precedence of all others, even that of child to parent. "For this cause shall a man leave father and mother, and shall cleave to his wife." (3) It makes the wedded pair one. They are to be one in their mutual self-giving. (4) This oneness is to last till death. For either husband or wife to give his or herself to another is to destroy this oneness and to become guilty of adultery.

2. Then Jesus counts those wrongfully married as violating this rule. This is the case with those who marry promiscuously. There are those who flit from husband to husband and from wife to wife as a bird flits from one branch of a tree to another. Such surely come under the condemnation of this rule. In fact, if Matthew quotes Jesus correctly, he frowns upon the remarriage of the divorced, unless they have been divorced for unfaithfulness. I know that this is a controverted question. I know also that there are those who argue that there is a moral equivalent of adultery. Nor am I denying that such may be the case. But the words of Jesus are very explicit: "Whosoever shall put away his wife, except it be for fornication, and shall marry another, committeth adultery." There is no doubt that those who marry promiscuously come under the condemnation of this rule. This is doubtless the case also of those who marry for any base reason upon which God could not smile.

Naturally, I am aware that there are those who are making a fair success of their marriage relationship, who according to this rule had no right to marry. What are these to do about it? They are to continue as they are, leaving their past to the tender mercies of God. To undo the past would be impossible. It would work more ill than good. Two wrongs can never make a right. This high ideal of marriage set forth by Jesus is intended to prevent rather than to cure. I am convinced that if we should take our Lord seriously in this matter, and diligently teach our children his conception of marriage, it would tend to their highest happiness and would prevent endless tragedy.

3. But this rule may not only be broken by the married, but by the unmarried as well. Unchastity on the part of one who is single is recognized as a breach of this law. Not only is this the case, but here again Jesus goes behind the overt act to the motive. "Whosoever looketh on a woman to lust after her hath committed adultery with her already in his heart." That does not mean that all sexual desire is wrong. It does mean that when the unclean desire is welcomed, brooded over, and only fails to become an act for lack of opportunity, this is to be guilty of adultery.

Here, then, is what is forbidden: unfaithfulness on the part of husband or wife, promiscuous marriages, unchastity in thought and deed.

II

Why is adultery forbidden?

Remember that nothing is either right or wrong in itself. If adultery is wrong, it is not wrong because this dusty old code forbids it. It is not wrong because it is frowned upon by Jesus and by the writers of the New Testament. It is not wrong because Puritanic preachers condemned it. It is wrong, if at all, because it is humanly hurtful. If it seeks our highest good and refuses to war against our highest happiness, then all our condemnation will not make it wrong. If a bottle contains pure milk, even to label that bottle with a cross-bones and skull will not change the milk into poison. Even so, no condemnation on our part can change an essential good into an evil.

But, on the other hand, if adultery is wrong in itself, if it is humanly hurtful, then all our defense of it will not make it otherwise. If it is wrong, then we cannot make it right by glossing it over with pleasing words. We cannot make it right by calling it self-expression. We cannot even make it right by calling it love. We can no more do this than we can cover up filth with snow and thereby make it pure. Is adultery then right, or is it wrong? Is it humanly hurtful or is it humanly helpful?

1. Consider, first, the breaches of this rule that are usually regarded as least harmful. Here, for instance, is a man pledged to no woman, and a woman pledged to no man. Perhaps they have both thrown off the restraints of religion. They do not consider themselves bound by any moral code. They are young and eager. They are convinced that they have a perfect right to live their own lives. If they agree together to enter into this experience, whose business is it? If they decide of their own free will thus to give themselves to each other, what is the harm?

Well, to begin with, in a society like ours, such conduct calls for secrecy. It drives us into the shadows and compels us to love the dark. This in itself works harm. The wisest teacher that it has been my privilege to know used to haunt his students with this word, "Don't do things on the sly." He was aware of the fact that we work injury to ourselves the moment we have to shroud our conduct in secrecy. This is true, in the first place, because the need of secrecy turns loose the nemesis of fear upon our track. If we have something to conceal, there is always a nagging fear that somebody will discover our secret. We are likely to be constantly on the run. The wise man was right when he said, "The guilty flee when no man pursueth." To live in fear is to live in wretchedness.

Then, no matter how emancipated we are, this practice tends to bring with it a sense of guilt. This is often the case with those who think that they have broken with all moral codes. Here is a story that I clipped from a Washington paper several months ago. It tells of a very modern young couple who defied this ancient code. She, according to her own opinion, was a thoroughly emancipated young woman, he an emancipated young man. But somehow they could not see it through. They were found one day locked in each other's arms in their gas-filled apartment. On the table was this letter written by the woman. "We have been accustomed to laugh, Fred and I, at the moral code as a set of man-made rules to frighten timid folks into being good. But we have learned through our own experience that the wages of sin is death, yea, many times worse than death, hell on earth." This is an extreme case, I know. But the failure that these two very modern young people made is an indication that adultery is not a safe foundation upon which to build your house of happiness.

Not only does this practice tend to give a sense of guilt and fear, but often the fears it arouses become tragic realities. Again and again the light is turned on, to our own shame and sorrow, as well as to that of others. This is the case, for one reason, because no contraceptive is a hundred per cent efficient. The truthfulness of this is seen when we face the fact that fifty thousand unmarried mothers are registered in the United States every year. It is realized also when we face the further fact that ten thousand girls die every year from illegal operations. Grim specters, therefore, stalk the road of the adulterer. Again and again these specters become tragic realities.

Then this course is dangerous because it lessens your chances for marriage. This is especially true in the case of the girl. The more a man asks her to give before marriage, the less likely he is to play the game according to the rules, and to keep his part of the bargain. The more she gives before marriage, the less likely she is to marry. The more she gives, the more likely she is to be left in jealousy and bitterness, while her companion-in-pleasure goes on to fresh conquests.

Not only does this evil lessen your chances of marriage; it also lessens your chances of making a success of this high relationship once you have entered into it. The man or the woman who has been promiscuous before marriage will find it very difficult to leave off the practice after marriage. You have also weakened your chances, even if you marry the one who has shared your extra-marital relations. Marriage is a high and exacting relationship always. But if a couple have reached the climax before they have really begun, the difficulties are increased. If they have passed through this experience in advance, they enter marriage with mutual distrust. If a question should arise, either would find it doubly easy to believe that one who disregarded this rule before marriage would disregard it afterwards. All in all, then, this practice, even on the part of those not bound to anyone else, is uniformly hurtful.

2. That adultery does harm to those who are married, almost all of us are ready to admit. To say the least, the husband who is unfaithful is a cheat; the same is true of the wife. We cannot thus cheat without hurting someone else. As a rule, we wreck our homes. Too often, we rob not only each other, but our children as well. Our reformatories are largely filled with those who are the shattered fragments of such broken homes. We have no right thus to cheat our children, ourselves, and society as a whole.

There are two conceptions of marriage that are fighting for supremacy today. There is the conception popularized by the cheaper elements of Hollywood. With these, it is about as smart to change from one mate to another as to change costumes. Then there is the Christian conception, in harmony with which certain prosaic souls may continue living together till they celebrate their golden wedding. Which is right? If you convince me that marriage à la Hollywood makes for a higher happiness on the part of husband and wife, gives children a better chance, makes a finer contribution to society, then I shall say that it is right. But I am convinced that the opposite is the case. Therefore, I say again that those in the marriage relationship who violate this code wrong both themselves and others.

3. Finally, we can realize something of the evil that the violation of this code involves by asking what would be the results if it were disregarded altogether. Such a course would surely result in the ruin of the individual, the destruction of the home, and the destruction of society. This is not mere supposition. More than one nation has been rotted down by this evil. Now since a total disregard of this law is a sure way to death, we ought to avoid it. No single one of us has the right to take a

course that, if taken by all, would mean the wrecking of our individual and national life. Since adultery hurts by leaving a sense of guilt, by dogging our steps with fear; since it robs us in some measure of our chances to marry, and of our chances to make a success of marriage; since it wars against the home, against childhood, and against society as a whole; it is a wrong. And since it is a wrong, we have no right to indulge in it.

III

How can we keep clean?

1. Face the fact that cleanliness is desirable. We find ourselves in situations at times when this does not seem to be the case. A young man told me some time ago that he had listened to vile stories told him by his companions, until he became actually ashamed of his own lack of experience. Finally he had his fling. From this he came with no sense of guilt at first, but rather with pride in the fact that he now had a story to tell as vile as that of his fellows. But there came a time when he was ashamed. At our best we know that it is better to be clean than unclean. All of us prefer cleanliness on the part of those we marry, whether we are men or women.

2. Believe that cleanliness is possible. No man is compelled to be unclean. I am not forgetting the fact that the sex urge is about the strongest that we know. But in spite of that fact, no man is compelled, I repeat, to be unclean. If that is not true, then we are not responsible for our own deeds. But every man knows that he is responsible. When we do wrong and face the fact that it is wrong, there is far more hope than if we do wrong and excuse ourselves by soft lies. To say that uncleanness is a necessity is to become morally color-blind. It is to put out the eyes of the soul.

3. Cultivate the habit of clean thinking. This evil, as all others, begins with wrong thinking. In order to avoid this wrong thinking, avoid those pastimes and companionships that make impure thinking all but inevitable. There are not a few shows that one would be the better for not seeing. Not every man can keep clean thoughts and engage in certain forms of the modern dance. Possibly the most fruitful source of unclean thinking in our day is promiscuous kissing, "necking" as it is called. It does not take much kissing of the lips of an unloved girl to kiss all the sweetness out. For a girl to scatter her favors broadcast is to cheapen herself and to hurt others.

4. Steer clear of intoxicants. Liquor tends at once to inflame desire and to weaken resistance. It gives a greater eagerness to say yes, and lessens the capacity to say no. As stated in our last message, it dopes Dr. Jekyl, and stimulates Mr. Hyde. Diana herself is capable of safeguarding her virtue only so long as she is sober.

5. Fall in love with somebody that is worth loving. I knew a young chap years ago who, faced by this temptation, said frankly, "I am in love with a girl on whose purity I would stake my life. I am not going to rob myself of giving what I demand on my wedding day." If such a love has not come into your life, then be in love with an ideal. For the sake of the one that you hope is coming to meet you in the future years, keep yourself in reserve. Spare yourself the tragedy of coming to the supreme experience of life with little or nothing to give.

6. Finally, claim a vital Christian experience. This will help in two very positive ways.

(1) It will give you a high sense of personal worth. It will call you, in the language of Tennyson, to be loyal to the royal in yourself. "Know ye not," said Paul, "that your body is the temple of the Holy Spirit." It is said that in South Africa a man stopped one day to witness a marble game that was

being played by a group of boys. He noticed that these marbles flashed and sparkled in the sunlight. His curiosity was aroused. Upon investigation, he found, to his amazement, that these boys were playing marbles with diamonds. Thus the South Africa diamond mines were discovered. Now diamonds may make good marbles, but they are made for something better.

There is a story of a certain minister who made his way to a cabin far in the mountains of East Tennessee. It was summertime and the cabin door was propped open by a scarred and battered book. The minister saw that this book was a masterpiece of the bookbinder's art, though it was now ugly and tarnished. The contents of this book amazed him even more, for it was the Bible. Yet these people could find no better use for this work of art, for the words of the prophets, the songs of the poets, the story of the cross, than to use it to prop open the door of a tumbledown cabin. Christianity braces us for clean living by calling us to respect ourselves as the temples of the Holy Spirit.

(2) Then religion helps one to keep clean by bringing a sense of God. Here is a young man away from home. He is in an enervating atmosphere. He is faced by circumstances where impurity is

easy and purity hard. To be unclean is the path to promotion. To be clean is the path to demotion and imprisonment. But he triumphs because he is undergirded by a bracing sense of God. His words come to us thrillingly across years. "Can I do this great evil and sin against God?" By this he means that he cannot do this evil. His assertion is, in a sense, a positive prayer. He is fixing his gaze, not upon his temptation, but upon his Deliverer. This is the way of victory. "This I say, walk in the Spirit, and ye shall not fulfil the lusts of the flesh."

But suppose you have failed to avail yourself of these helps. Suppose that you are, even now, grieving over the fact that you no longer wear "the white flower of a blameless life," what then? Just remember that no failure need be final but the failure to repent, and start anew. Remember also that Jesus is ready to say to you what, in the long ago, he said to another who had failed: "Go, and sin no more."

VIII

RESPECT THE RIGHTS OF OTHERS

Thou shalt not steal.

EXODUS 20: 15

I

WHAT IS IT TO STEAL?

1. To steal is to take by stealth or force that which rightly belongs to another. This is true whether the values stolen are tangible or intangible; whether they are values that we see, or values that we do not see. Stealing is thus an aggressive something. It requires activity on the part of the thief. Often this activity is dangerous, putting in peril the freedom, and even the life, of the thief. But whether the stealing is dangerous or safe, if we wrench values either from the hand or the heart of a brother, we are guilty of the violation of this rule.

2. To steal is to withhold from our fellows that which they have a right to expect at our hands. Our lives interlock one with the other. Seriously to ask the question, "Am I my brother's keeper?" is to show disregard for the rights of others. No man but a potential thief would ask such a question. Every man owes a debt to his fellows. To refuse to pay that debt is to violate this law. A thief, therefore, may be very active and aggressive. He may give himself to days and nights of strenuous toil. He may also be merely passive. He may fold his hands in idleness like the sluggard and say, "a little more sleep and a little more slumber."

> I never cut my neighbor's throat,
>   My neighbor's purse I never stole,
> I never spoiled his house and land,
>   But God have mercy on my soul!
> For I am haunted night and day
>   By all the deeds I have not done;
> O unattempted loveliness!
>   O costly valor never won!

Therefore, whether the stealing is active or passive, whether we take that which is another's, or withhold that which we ought to give to another, we are guilty of the violation of this rule.

II

Now stealing is fascinating. I doubt if we have ever really considered just how fascinating it is. It is estimated that the violation of this rule costs the United States more than ten billions of dollars every year. Any practice that can command so much money must have a powerful appeal. Then, of course, we realize that the stealing of tangible values represents only a small fraction of all the values that are stolen year by year. In dealing, therefore, with stealing, we are dealing with a practice that has tremendous fascination. Why is this the case?

1. Stealing is fascinating because it is one way of getting something that we are eager to possess. Many of us take a pride in wanting what we want when we want it. We cannot be bothered by resisting our desires. Here is a bank, for instance. In that bank is money, a vast sum. We desire to possess that money for ourselves. We feel that, if it were only ours, it would mean high-powered cars. It would mean freedom from toil. It would minister to our pride. It would bring us power. So compelling is the spell that this money casts upon us that we rob the bank. Stealing is one way of getting something that we want.

2. Then stealing is tremendously fascinating because it is not only a way of getting something that we desire, but of getting that something for nothing. Now there is no measuring the fascination that the prospect of getting something for nothing has for certain types of men and women. Often we will gladly pay twice as much for an article as it is worth because we think we are getting something for nothing. Barnum said long ago that the American people loved to be humbugged. He need not have limited himself to the American people. It would seem that this is a characteristic of the race. The countless millions of skin-games that have been played upon humanity through the centuries are an evidence of our eagerness to get something for nothing.

Take gambling, for instance. There are those who argue that the gambler is also a thief. I would not put it so strongly as that. But there is no doubt that the thief and gambler have much in common. In the first place, they are the victims of a common blindness. They have both made up their minds that they can get something for nothing. Though they are aware that they live in a world where men reap what they sow, yet these flatter themselves into believing that they are exceptions to the rule. Silly souls like the other fellow may be caught, but not they. They are wise enough to gather grapes of thorns and figs of thistles.

Then the thief and the gambler are alike in that they are actuated by a common motive. What makes gambling a passion for so many people? *American Business* declares that our gambling bill is six billions per year. We spend one billion each year on foreign sweepstakes. Why does gambling grapple its victims with hooks of steel? Why does it hold those addicted to it with a tenacious grip like that of liquor or of drugs? The answer is simple. It holds out the lure of getting something for nothing. Now this is also the lure of stealing. Both thief and gambler, therefore, are strange mixtures of moral stupidity and rascality. For the man who thinks he can permanently get something for nothing is a bit of a fool. The man who wants to get something for nothing is a bit of a rascal, and has in him the making of a thief.

3. The final reason I give for the fascination of stealing is that it ministers to our conceit. Here again the thief and the gambler are alike. The successful thief, as the successful gambler, is usually a confirmed egotist. By outsharping his fellows, he has, in a sense, put them in their place. By getting

values for nothing for which others have to sweat, he has shown his superiority. He can drive high-powered cars with soft palms, while others, poor nit-wits, have to sweat and get their palms calloused in order to have such privileges. Of course, many thieves have been caught, but not he. He knows more than all others that have gone before. In fact, wisdom will perish with his bones. No wonder he swaggers.

Now this sense of being a bit smarter than one's fellows belongs not only to the gangster, the embezzler, and the successful gambler; it belongs also to many thieves who steal by simply doing nothing. It belongs often to the chap whose home and business are safeguarded by the community, but who never makes any contribution to that community. A young husband and father said the other day, "I never go to church. I never contribute anything to the church." He said it as if it were a positive virtue. Those who know him realize that he could say the same thing about the Community Chest, and about all other enterprises of common interest. He seems to flatter himself that while others are paying their fare, he is managing to ride on a pass. Thus he glories in what should make his face burn with shame. Stealing, then, fascinates because it offers what men want. Not only so, but it offers this prize for nothing. Thus it satisfies some desires while, at the same time, it ministers to conceit.

III

WHAT are some of the common kinds of stealing that are prevalent today?

1. Take it on its positive side. Of course, there are those who steal material values. But we can pass over these lightly. I am not in the least uneasy that any here present will be pickpockets, embezzlers, or gangsters. The type of stealing that brings one into conflict with the law is not likely to appeal to many of us. But this, perhaps, is not so true of stealing within the law. For instance, I have known more than one churchman to take advantage of another's hard luck to put him to the wall. This type of stealing is more contemptible than that of the highwayman. The knight of the road does possess a certain kind of daring. But not even this can be claimed for those who steal within the law. He exposes himself to no danger at all.

For instance, one of the most despicable characters in the Old Testament, when he first comes upon the scene, is Jacob. He prides himself on the fact that he can live by his wits. One day his big hungry brother comes in from the chase. Jacob is cooking dinner. The savory odor of these steaming lentils comes to the nostrils of Esau with a compelling appeal. "Feed me that red stuff," he begs.

"All right," says the wily Jacob. "But first, sell me your birthright."

"Take it," says Esau. "I am about to die." He then sits down and eats and drinks and rises up and goes his way. But this sane Book does not count Jacob as having bought his brother's birthright. It rather counts him as having stolen it. But he was never arrested. He stole within the law.

Then, we steal no less when we take from another values that are not material. Take reputation, for example. My reputation is the capital upon which I do business. Just in proportion as you rob me of my good name, in that same proportion do you rob me of my usefulness. This you do without helping yourself in the least. The same is true if I thus rob you. This is what makes this kind of stealing so utterly devilish. It hurts others without helping one's self. It is like stealing bread from the hungry with no better purpose than to throw it into the sewer.

"He that filches from me my good name,

Robs me of that which not enriches him,
And makes me poor indeed."

Then we can rob another of those inner supports
without which life falls into ruins. David Hume
thus robbed his mother of her faith. When she
came to old age, she was utterly desolate. We can
rob another of expectation and of hope. There are
some people that have a veritable genius for bringing encouragement. By being what they are, they
bring hope. Then there are others that have a genius
in the opposite direction. However blue our sky
when we meet these, it is full of scudding clouds
and tempest when they go their way. There ought
to be a special kind of prison in which to lock those
that wilfully rob their fellows of their faith, and
courage, and hope.

2. But possibly the most dangerous form of stealing is the passive. We can steal by wrenching
treasures from a brother's hand or heart. But we
can also steal by simply doing nothing. Take, for
instance, the man who refuses to pay what he owes
in terms of dollars and cents. The man who borrows money without the expectation of paying it
back is a thief. The man who buys or borrows in
good faith and refuses to pay when he can pay is a

thief. There was a sophomore in Duke University years ago who bought a set of books from a junior who had just finished with them. It so happened that he bought them on a credit. Near commencement the year following, the student who sold the books, now a senior, asked payment. The junior, who had now used the books for a whole year and no longer needed them, gathered them up and flung them at the feet of his creditor, saying in indignation, "It makes me mad for a man to dun me. It used to make my father mad when men dunned him." What a hero! No, we say rather, what a contemptible thief!

But we owe money not only when we have made a bargain, but also no less when nothing has been bought, or when no loan has been made. This fact has been recognized through the centuries. A certain prophet accused his fellow citizens of robbery in the long ago. This he did, not because they had taken treasure to which they had no right. They had only withheld the tithe. It is not my present purpose to say whether it is right for you to tithe or not. But what I do say is: no man has a right to live in any community and refuse to make some contribution to that community. This he ought to do both in terms of money, if he has it, and in terms of personal service as well.

Jesus once told a story in which both the positive and the passive types of stealing rub elbows with each other. "A certain man went down from Jerusalem to Jericho, and fell among thieves, which stripped him of his raiment, and wounded him, and departed, leaving him half dead." The robbers who did this were of the aggressive type. They hid in the fastness of the mountains and waited for their helpless victim. When he came their way, with a total disregard for his rights, with a total disregard for those who would wait with heartache and fear that night for his homecoming, they robbed him and wounded him, and left him to his fate.

But these cruel thugs were not the only robbers on the highway that day. As this poor fellow lay bleeding by the roadside, a priest came by, then a Levite. These were decent, law-abiding, religious men. Therefore, they did not ride over this helpless man. They did not rob him of what few shreds of clothing the brigands had left him. They only passed by on the other side, and left him to die. By so doing, they put themselves in the prisoner's dock along with the bloody-handed men who had struck him down and had stolen his treasure. We may steal aggressively, but the most insidious form of stealing, and the most dangerous, is the passive type. This is the case because such stealing often makes repentance impossible by relieving us of all sense of guilt.

IV

WHAT is wrong with stealing? Of course, it is all but useless to ask that question. We recognize the fact that it works at least a twofold injury.

1. It works injury to others. This is the case whether one steals a man's money, or steals other values that are intangible. We recognize the wrong of stealing especially when we are the victims. When Jacob robbed Esau, it would seem that he did the job without a pang. In fact, I think he looked upon the transaction as quite shrewd and brillaint. But when a bit later he himself was robbed by Laban, he was outraged. "Thou hast beguiled me," he said in amazed indignation. He thought of himself as a pitiful innocent that had been tragically wronged. We cannot steal from others, in any fashion, without hurting the one from whom we steal.

2. But the greatest injury that is done by the thief is to himself. His victim may suffer, but often his suffering is comparatively very slight. We

may steal from the government, for instance, without causing the nation to totter. Surely many have tried this out. We may beat our way on the street-car with the smug conviction that seven cents will matter very little to so strong a corporation. In this we shall be in a sense entirely right. A big corporation can get along quite well without the seven cents. But it is equally true that you and I cannot get on quite well without being honest.

Thieving, then, in its mildest forms, cheats the cheater. At best, it makes the one who practices it a parasite. That, in itself, is tragedy. No man can really get away with stealing. If no one else finds him out, his sin will. In fact, the most pathetic thief is the one who is getting away with his dishonesty. Sin is always a failure, but it never fails so disastrously as when it succeeds. It is always deadly, but it never kills so brutally as when it seems to give life. The thief that is caught pays a terrible price. But the thief that is not caught often pays a bigger still. He convinces himself that he can beat the game and bring good out of evil. Thus he becomes morally color-blind, and runs past his capacity to repent.

V

WHAT then shall we do with this sane rule?

If we are wise, we shall seek to obey it. We shall seek to obey it by having a wholesome respect for the rights of others. We shall face the fact that we are debtors. "A gentleman," said Bernard Shaw, "puts more into life than he takes out of it." To be honest men, we must at least seek to put as much into life as we take out. I doubt if any of us pay for our keep, but we must do our best in that direction. To fail, is to fall under the condemnation of this rule.

But suppose one has already violated it, then what? I answer in the language of Paul. "Let him that stole, steal no more." But this rule goes deeper than that. It is not enough for some to quit; they must make restitution. One day Jesus paid a visit to Jericho. Among those who sought to serve on the reception committee was an outcast named Zacchaeus. But his respectable fellows would have none of him. Therefore, in order to get to see the Master, he was compelled to climb into a tree. When Jesus came by and saw him, he said, "Zacchaeus, make haste and come down, for today I must abide at thy house." And we read that Zacchaeus came down and received him joyfully. But that reception involved more than that. It involved the disgorging of his ill-gotten gains. "If I have taken anything from any man by false accusation," he vowed, "I restore him fourfold." Then, and only then, did Jesus say, "This day is salvation come to this house!"

I am told that, years ago, a wealthy bachelor who belonged to a prominent church in Chicago went to hear a certain man preach. He was brought under deep conviction of sin. But when he went alone to pray, an unrighted wrong came before him and made real prayer impossible. He had stolen the love and confidence of a girl, and having used her, had cast her aside. He realized that there could be no peace till he had righted that wrong. When he went back to his home town, he found that the girl had died; but their child, a boy, was in an orphans' home. He found that boy, and brought him back to Chicago with him.

"Son," he said, the first night at home, "do you think you could forgive your father, though he had done your mother a great wrong?"

"I don't know," came the answer.

"Then put your arms around me and call me father." And this man declared that he found forgiveness when he felt the clinging arms of this boy.

Here, then, is a rule that calls us to respect the

rights of others. If we have robbed others, it calls for restitution in so far as is within our power. Its demands, therefore, are so high that we need God in our hearts in order to fulfill them. In fact, we must have him, if we are to keep this rule in its fullness.

IX

CONTROL YOUR TONGUE

*Thou shalt not bear false wit-
ness against thy neighbor.*

EXODUS 20: 16

❈

To some this is a rasping rule that seems downright insulting. It tends to point an accusing finger at us and to shake its ugly fist in our faces. This is especially true when we realize that it is speaking directly to ourselves. For instance, were I to go to any one of you at the close of this service, grip you by the arm, look you squarely in the eye, and say, "Thou shalt not bear false witness against thy neighbor," you would resent it. In fact, I would count myself fortunate if I should escape bodily injury. Not even the rule against stealing sounds more brutally insulting than this against bearing false witness.

But there are circumstances that could take all the

harshness out of this rasping rule and give it a touch of real tenderness. Suppose that you happen to be the victim rather than the offender. Suppose you are being tortured by venom-tongued talebearers that are making your life miserable, then what? If, knowing all this, I should go to you, run my arm through yours, and say, "I am sorry for what you are suffering. Your neighbor has no right to bear false witness against you," your attitude would be entirely different. Under these circumstances, this rule would become as kindly and comforting as the protecting arms of a mother to a tired and frightened child.

I

WHAT do we mean by bearing false witness?

1. Its first and simplest meaning is the giving of false evidence in a court of law. The primary purpose of law courts is to guarantee justice between man and man. Before justice can be done, judge and jury must know the facts. In order for them to know the facts, there must be reliable witnesses. A false witness may defeat the ends of justice. He may, by his false testimony, rob his neighbor of his property. He may rob him of his freedom. He may even rob him of his life. A false witness, therefore,

is always a liar. He may be, also, a thief or a murderer.

2. But false witnessing is not confined to courts of law. We are always bearing witness for or against our neighbor, whether we ever take the witness stand or not. To testify to that regarding our neighbor which is not true, is to be guilty of the violation of this rule, whether in court or not. The one who peddles malicious gossip is a false witness. The one who slanders by telling what is untrue, or what is only half true, is guilty of bearing false witness.

3. Not only is this true, but we can bear false witness against our neighbor without making any positive statement at all. In fact, some of the most subtle and cowardly forms of slander are made in this fashion. We can bear false witness in a most damning way by merely asking questions. Satan, in the immortal drama of Job, is a master of this art. When God commends Job by saying, "Hast thou considered my servant Job, that there is none like him in the earth, a man . . . that feareth God, and escheweth evil?" what answer does Satan make? He makes no positive accusation against Job. He does not say flatly that he is a hypocrite and a crook. He is far too keen to make so crude a declaration. Instead, he asks a question: "Does Job fear God for

naught?" How shrewd, and how utterly devilish!

The shrewdness of this method of slander is seen in the fact that it is at once effective and safe. Had Satan declared that Job had stolen a camel, or that he had murdered a neighbor, he might have been called upon to prove the truthfulness of his declaration. This might have got him into trouble. But by asking a question, he put Job under a cloud without incurring any risk at all. Nobody can punish us for merely asking a question. Does John Smith pay his debts? Is Tom Brown's wife true to him? Here is a very popular girl. Young men are constantly seeking her company. But is she straight? By thus asking questions, we can get all the effect of bearing false witness without incurring any of its dangers.

Not only did Satan show his keenness by asking a question rather than making an assertion, but he asked a question to which nobody could give an authoritative answer. Had he asked, "Did Job kill his wife?" that might have been answered with accuracy. But he did not question Job's outward conduct. That was an open book. He was quite willing to concede that, so far as the eye could see, Job was a thoroughly decent and good man. He was willing to agree that God was entirely right in his estimate, so long as one looked only upon the surface. To see what a scoundrel Job was it was necessary to look within. What was wrong was his motives. He had been decent all right, but it was at a price. "Does Job serve God for naught?" Certainly not. He is good for what he can get out of it. Therefore, though sound on the outside, he is rotten within. And neither Job nor his friends can prove Satan is wrong.

4. Then we can bear false witness by saying never a word. We can remain as dumb as an oyster, and yet be guilty of violating this rule. For instance, when we hear a disreputable story about another, and know that story to be a lie, and yet remain silent, we are guilty of bearing false witness against our neighbor. In fact, we can be guilty, even while defending in a patronizing and half-hearted way. This is the case where we

"Damn with faint praise, assent with civil leer,
    And without sneering, teach the rest to sneer;
Willing to wound, and yet afraid to strike,
Just hint a fault, and hesitate dislike."

5. Another way of bearing false witness is flattery. Now, I am not talking about a just and honest compliment. We all like to be complimented.

I am quite sure, too, that few of us compliment as much as we could, and yet stay within the truth. I am convinced also that the machinery of the world would run far more smoothly if it were more frequently oiled by the fine lubricant of appreciation. But the man who is everlastingly broadcasting compliments is apt to be a bit of a liar. The chances, too, are great that he is taking his object for a fool. This he is doing, not to help the other, but to further his own selfish ends. "The words of his mouth were smoother than butter, but war was in his heart. His words were softer than oil, yet were they drawn swords."

There are those whose compliments we never think of taking seriously—that is, except when they are complimenting ourselves. In this case, we say to ourselves, "I know that George is a habitual liar. I know that he is constantly flattering folks to bend them to his purpose. But my case is an exception. What he says about me is true." Thus he takes us in. I knew a very intelligent man who prided himself on the fact that nobody could flatter him. A certain book agent learned of his peculiarity, and went at once to see him. Having been admitted to his presence, he began his conversation by complimenting him on the fact that he was immune to flattery. Thus approached, he bought his book at once. Perhaps there was nothing wrong in this approach, but the persistent flatterer is a bearer of false witness.

6. Finally, the faultfinder comes under the condemnation of this rule. "Judge not," said Jesus. What did he mean by this word? He is certainly not forbidding our reaching some conclusions with regard to the worth or worthlessness of those with whom we have to do. We cannot help reaching some decision as to the good or evil, the sincerity or insincerity, of those about us. At our first service together you began to make up your mind as to what kind of man I am. I did the same with regard to you. This is at once inevitable and necessary. We cannot conduct the business of living in a sensible fashion except we decide as to the good or bad character of those with whom we do business.

Jesus calls for such a decision in the very chapter in which he warns not to judge. "Give not that which is holy unto the dogs, neither cast ye your pearls before swine." What does the Master mean by dogs and swine? His words are not to be taken literally. He is not speaking of actual dogs and hogs. He is rather speaking of people that are doggish and hoggish in their natures. But how are we to obey this precept against casting pearls before swine, unless we reach some conclusions as to who is swinish and who is not?

That which is forbidden, then, by this command is not judging, but faultfinding, the habit of seeking for the worst in our fellows instead of for the best. Such a course is forbidden because it leads inevitably to bearing false witness. This is true because the man that seeks for the worst will find it. This holds in every department of life. If we seek for the worst in the world of nature, we will find it. If we seek for the worst in the church, we shall find it. If we seek for the worst in a neighbor, we shall find it. And, just in proportion as we find the worst and fix our gaze upon it, in that same proportion shall we fail to find the best. Our report of our neighbor, therefore, will not be a true witness, but a false.

What does the vulture find when he flies over a landscape? Perchance a dead possum under a thorn bush. This does not mean that that bit of carrion is all of which this landscape can boast. It may be green with grass and colorful with flowers. It may be a-sparkle with dew and sweet with the song of birds. But the vulture misses all of these, because he is looking only for something that is rotten. We may look with similar eyes upon our fellows. But, if such is the case, in so doing we are sure to bring back a false report. We shall agree with the cynic in Ecclesiastes that mankind is uniformly bad, and that the crooked can never be made straight. That is the supreme slander. There is no deadlier way of bearing false witness against one's neighbor than that.

II

THE violation of this rule, as well as that of all the others, hurts its victim. There is no measuring the pain, the heartache, and the tears that the bearing of false witness has caused. Such a man robs his victim of treasures that are more priceless than life. A few years ago, a certain minister in Texas had to give up his pastorate on account of ill health. In order to make a living he rented a bit of land from a wealthy farmer. Soon this farmer, because of his great confidence in his tenant, began to trust him with considerable sums of money. One pay-day he was returning from the bank with the sum of five thousand dollars. At a turn of the road, a highway-man stepped from the bushes, leveled a gun in his face, and called for the money. The minister did not deny possession of the money. What he said was this: "All I have to leave my boys is this team of mules and my good name. That good name is worth more to me than my life. Therefore, if you want this money enough to murder me, shoot. You will get it in no other way." This man, as many others, valued his good name more than he valued his life.

Then the false witness hurts his victim by making it easier for him to go wrong and harder for him to go right. It has been well said that if one gives a dog a bad name, he will justify it. How many folk go wrong because nobody expects anything better of them! On the other hand, there is nothing so bracing as confidence. Paul had a way of addressing those to whom he wrote as saints. After this, he often had to utter some sharp criticisms. But, by so addressing them, he gave them something to live up to. He thus fixed their gaze upon their highest possibilities. He thus undergirded them by his confidence. It is far harder to go wrong, and far easier to go right, if we know ourselves to be trusted.

Finally, slander often embitters those who would otherwise be friendly. Do you remember Nick Burr in one of Ellen Glasgow's stories? He was a fine, clean, hard-working young chap. By sheer grit and merit he was making his way to the top. But he was slandered. The slander was so cunning that it was believed, even by the woman that loved him and that he loved. This inflicted a wound that was never healed. "They have lied on me," he said to her fiercely, "and you believed it, and I can never forgive you. And, as for the liar, may God in his just mercy damn him." It is awful to be a possessor of a hate like that. But it is more awful still to make a kindly man into such a hater.

2. Then the false witness does something to his hearer. Scientists used to argue whether there could be sound where there was no ear to hear. Certainly there could be no bearing of false witness without a hearer. When the malicious gossip gets to broadcasting, if nobody tuned in, he would soon go off the air. But some encourage him by giving him a hearing. Of course, these would never think of saying the cruel things that he says. But the fact that they tune in shows their kinship with him. If you should come to me tomorrow with a lovely diamond ring and say, "Here is a beautiful ring I want you to keep for me. I stole it last week. You may have a chance to sell it; in case you do, I will make it worth your while." You would not make such a proposition, except you believed me to be a thief.

Such a man is called in the language of the under-world a "fence." The receiver of stolen goods is just as guilty as the thief. Years ago in one of our colleges, authorities broke open a young man's trunk and found some sixty watches. I wonder if our premises were searched how many stolen reputations would be found? To listen is to share the guilt of the liar.

3. Finally, the false witness strikes his deadliest blow at himself. This is the case because he gets paid in his own coin. "Judge not, that ye be not judged. For with what judgment ye judge, ye shall be judged: and with what measure ye mete, it shall be measured to you again." "By thy words," said Jesus again, "shalt thou be justified, and by thy words shalt thou be condemned." If we are harsh in our judgments of our brother, the chances are that he is going to be harsh in his judgments of us. As a general rule, we get what we give. If your hand is against every man, every man's hand is likely to be against you. Complaining that no man ever has a kind word to say of you, is another way of saying that you never have a kind word to say of another. "With what measure ye mete, it shall be measured to you again." That is true in this world;

it is equally true in all worlds. To bear false witness, therefore, is to wrong one's self.

Not only is this the case because we get what we give, but because this habit brings in its wake a terrible blindness. This is the case because the more keen we become to the faults of others, the more dead we become to our own. Jesus told this story: One day a man met a neighbor, and said, "By the way, my friend, there is a mote in your eye. Stand still, and let me remove it." But this friend looked his critic over, and gave this sane answer, "There is a beam, a whole log, in yours. Let me remove that." Thus the more conscious we become of the faults of others, the more unconscious do we become of our own. The more the false witness tears his neighbor down, the more he feels that he builds himself up. Therefore, he hangs a ball and chain about his soul, and makes any progress toward the light an impossibility.

III

How, then, shall we keep this rule?

1. First, let us realize how ill-fitted the best of us are for assuming the rôle of judge. That is a position for which God, and God alone, is adequate. How often we are mistaken, even when we are sure

that we know the facts! How often our knowledge is pitifully partial! Even when we know the facts, how impossible it is to weigh all the motives that lie behind them. How many times, after judging harshly, have we said, "If I had only known, I should never have been so heartless and so cruel!"

2. It is also well to remember that, when we know certain soiled pages in the life story of a neighbor, we have no right to point them out, except at the call of love. Sometimes love may lead us to expose a neighbor in order to save those that he might injure. But such cases are rare. As a rule we expose, not because we love, but because we are loveless. The Elder Son is a case in point. When he reminded his father that the Prodigal had wasted his substance with harlots, he reached a veritable climax of meanness and cruelty. Beware of telling anything that will needlessly break somebody's heart.

"If you see a tall fellow ahead of the crowd,
  A leader of men walking fearless and proud,
  And know of a tale whose mere telling aloud
  Would cause his proud head to in anguish be bowed,
  It is a pretty good thing to forget it."

3. Finally, crowd out the evil by the good. The Apostle James in his terrific arraignment of the

tongue says, "The tongue is a fire." By this he is seeking to tell what a power for evil the tongue may become. Fire may be a most destructive something. But fire is not necessarily an evil. It is an evil only when it gets out of control. Otherwise it is a great good. It is such a great good that the ancients reckoned it as having been stolen from heaven. How comforting it is upon the hearthstone of home! How powerful it is! If all fires were to go out tonight, the machinery of the world would stop. My tongue may be that kind of a fire. It may heal, and help, and comfort. "Your words," said one of Job's friends, "have kept men on their feet." So may your words and mine.

It is, therefore, to this high use of words that this sane rule is calling. This week I had the pleasure of delivering the commencement address to the graduating class of Oklahoma City University. Among those who received their diplomas was a young man who is a hopeless cripple. How did he manage to get to the platform? When his name was called, one of his fellows gathered him in his arms, as if he had been a baby, and shared his strength with him. That brought a thrill. You will not be surprised to know that it was when these came that the applause was most thunderous.

There was a light in the face of the young man who was thus putting himself under the burden of his friend. To obey this rule is to know a similar joy. Therefore, "Thou shalt not bear false witness against thy neighbor."

X

MASTER YOUR DESIRES

Thou shalt not covet.

EXODUS 20: 17

I

THE WORD COVET AS USED IN THE BIBLE HAS more than one meaning. There is a sense in which covetousness is altogether right. One meaning of covet is to desire earnestly. For the Buddhist, heaven is the cessation of all desires. But for us such a state would not be heaven at all. It would only be the cemetery. There are certain values that we have a perfect right to desire with earnestness.

1. Every man has a right to covet an opportunity to work. No man can live a rich and full life who is an idler, whether his idleness is born of laziness or of lack of opportunity. To work is godlike.

"My father worketh even until now, and I work."
Every man, therefore, has a right to be a worker.
Not only so, but he has a right to work under conditions as wholesome as possible, and for a living
wage. Such an opportunity is not a matter of char-
ity, but of justice. The church has sometimes been
accused of being indifferent to man's physical needs.
It has been accused of making religion an opiate by
telling those that are cheated and oppressed that they
will "get their pie in the sky." They are, therefore,
to bear their present ills with the assurance that all
their wrongs will be righted by and by.

Now we regret to confess that this charge against
organized religion has in it some measure of truth.
In certain nations it has been conspicuously true.
The hostility to the church in Russia and Spain today is certainly born of the fact that for years the
church has taken the side of the oppressors. But in
so far as the church has done this, at any time or
place, it has been unchristian. Jesus was deeply concerned with the needs of the whole man. He was
concerned that the kingdom of heaven, the kingdom
of righteousness and justice, be established in the
here and now. This also must be our concern. The
man, therefore, who covets the right to work at a
wage that gives him and his some opportunity to

share the good things of life is coveting only that which is just.

2. Not only does every man have a right to work, but every man has a right to equip himself to do his work. I am quite sure that there are a great many young men and women in our colleges and universities that have no business there. They are not there because they desire to know, but because they are sent. But those who are eager to know, those who desire to "follow knowledge like a sinking star," have a right to an opportunity. The man, therefore, who covets knowledge is perfectly right in so doing.

3. Then every man has a right to covet the realization of his best possibilities as a Christian. "Covet earnestly," says Paul, "the best gifts." That means that we are earnestly to desire the very best that God has for us. We are to desire to be our best. We are also to desire to do our best. Jesus pronounces a blessing on all such. "Blessed are they that do hunger and thirst after righteousness." Blessed is the man that yearns to be good himself, and that yearns for that same rich benediction for his fellows. To covet, then, the knowledge of God, to yearn intensely for the triumph of his kingdom within one's heart and throughout the world, is altogether right.

Not only is it right for us to covet after this fashion, but to fail to do so is a mark of moral and spiritual sickness, if not of positive death. "Godliness with contentment is great gain." But there is a kind of contentment that is a dead loss. The Prodigal in the far country among the swine is not to be envied. But while his plight is pathetic enough, he has not yet reached the climax of calamity. This is the case because he is still tormented by home-loves and haunted by home-memories. He cannot forget that he was made for something better than to labor and to fellowship with hogs. But should he ever come to say to himself, "Well, this is not so good, but it is the best that I can do," then his situation would be hopeless. To be useless in a needy world is bad enough, but to become content with one's uselessness is worse still. To persuade ourselves that such a state is God's best for us spells disaster. When we reach that tragic position,

> "The lamp of our youth will be clean burnt out,
>   But we will subsist on the smell of it,
> And whatever we do, we will fold our hands
>   And suck our gums, and think well of it.
> Yes, we shall be perfectly pleased with ourselves,
>   And that is the perfectest hell of it."

II

But the word covet as used in our text means inordinate desire. That is, it means desire that is unlawful. There are many desires of this kind. Let us mention only a few that come under the condemnation of this rule.

1. This rule forbids our desiring that to which we have no right. "Thou shalt not covet," says this law. We are not to covet our neighbor's property, his house, his ox; we are not to covet his wife. But, lest some values might be left out, this law closes with the inclusive word, "Thou shalt not covet . . . anything that is thy neighbor's." That is, we have no right to desire to possess any value that belongs to our neighbor, without making our neighbor an adequate return. When, therefore, we look at our neighbor's car and say in our heart, "I wish that car were mine, even though my gain would be my neighbor's loss," then we are guilty of the violation of this rule. To covet is to desire that to which one has no right.

2. But covetousness goes deeper than this. To covet is to desire more than one needs, more than one can possibly use. I believe in private ownership of property. But I do not believe that any man has a right to own all the property there is. He has no

moral right to own that which is of no use to him, and which, but for his greediness, might be of service to another. Such a man becomes a mere dog in the manger. A dog, you know, does not eat hay, or oats, or corn. These are of no value to him. But he can sit in the manger and snap and snarl at the hungry horses and cattle, and thus prevent their eating. This snapping and snarling is his way of saying, "Keep off the grass." In our present world some wealthy men are exactly in that position. They themselves cannot possibly use what they have, and they are unwilling to make it of use to others. Their ownership, therefore, does not mean so much their right to enjoy as the right to keep their fellows from enjoying.

Do you remember Mr. Livingston in *Santa Claus' Partner?* Mr. Livingston was a very active and aggressive young business man. He had one overmastering ambition. He was bent on accumulating a fortune of a million dollars. Now the desire to be worth a million dollars is not bad, provided one has a right motive back of this desire. But why did this keen and strenuous human dynamo desire to be worth a million? Was it in order that he might help his fellows? Did he desire to build a hospital, or a college, or an orphanage? Not a bit of it.

"Why do you want to be worth a million?" a friend asked. "In order to be able to tell the other fellow to go to the devil," was his shocking answer. In speaking after this fashion he showed himself a covetous man. The man who desires more than he needs, more than he can possibly use, is covetous.

3. Finally, to covet is to put the secular above the spiritual. It is to put gain above God. It is to seek first to get hold upon things instead of seeking first the Kingdom of God and his righteousness. It is to be concerned more for material values than for human values. It is to put the saving of money above the saving of men. In a village where I was working years ago, the boys and girls were in some measure missing their opportunities for an education because of the inadequate building in which the school was held. I set out to get the patrons interested in the erecting of a new building. First, I got together a small committee of those who represented the wealth of the community. The richest man in the group was all enthusiasm for the enterprise. But there was one condition. "I will certainly help," he affirmed magnificently, "provided you show me that I will get a dividend."

There you have it! He was only interested in what would pay a dividend, not in terms of trained young men and women, but only in terms of dollars and cents. That is, he put money values first. That means he was avaricious. That means that he was in the grip of that love of money which Paul declared was the root of every kind of evil. The man who cares more for financial gains than he does for having a victorious church, a clean city, a wholesome community where boys and girls may have the best possible chance of growing into strong, God-fearing men and women—that man is covetous, and thus comes under the condemnation of this rule.

III

Now what is wrong with covetousness? What does it do to us that is harmful?

The writers of the Bible condemn it with one voice. They condemn it because they are sure that it works evil to those who give way to it. They reached their conviction, no doubt, because they had witnessed some of the wrecks that it had wrought. I was called a few years ago to see a woman who had taken bichloride of mercury. She did not take a sufficient quantity to kill her at once. But now, after eight days, she was dying a slow and ghastly death. She was literally rotting above ground. I have since been against the taking of bichloride of mercury. This is the case because I have seen what it will do. This is how the writers of the Bible reached their convictions. They have seen the ruin that it works.

What, then, is the harm of covetousness?

1. Covetousness kills contentment. It makes us fretful, feverish, and wretched. This is the case, for one reason, because it fixes our gaze on what we have not instead of upon what we really have. When I was a boy I used to feed the hogs. I would carry out a basket that contained at least a hundred ears of corn, and pour it all upon the ground. The supply was ample for the needs of all. But there was almost always one silly hog that would grab an ear and take up the hillside as if running for his life. How stupid! But what was more stupid still was this: another hog would at once turn his back on ninety-nine good ears and pursue his fleeing fellow. This he would do with squeals and whines as pitiful as tears. Being thus covetous, he was wretched in the presence of plenty. What a human hog!

You remember Ahab. One day he pouted into his palace, looking like a spoiled baby. He flung himself upon a divan, and turned his face to the wall. What was the matter? He had so set his

heart on a vineyard that belonged to somebody else
that his own hands seemed absolutely empty. The
Book of Esther tells a similar story. Everyone
knows Haman, but tends to forget everything about
him except that he was hanged. But Haman had
some fine qualities. He was a strong man. In
spite of the fact that he was a foreigner, he worked
his way up till he became the most powerful man in
the Persian Empire. Everybody looked up to him.
Everybody did obeisance to him. That is, everybody
except one. There was one stiff-necked Jew named
Mordecai who refused to bow. This so enraged
Haman that he forgot all the thousands who did
bow. He so fixed his attention on the one thing that
he lacked that he made himself miserable, and ended
by getting himself hanged. Covetousness makes for
wretchedness.

2. Then covetousness leads to wrongdoing. Covetousness is a fountain from which flow many poi-
sonous streams. The one who violates this rule is
likely to violate every other. Covetousness often
leads to lying, to bearing false witness. To covet
the wife of another is to become an adulterer. To
covet another's goods is, at times, to become a legal
thief. It is, at other times, to take that which one
may own according to the law of man, but which is

another's according to the law of fair play and decency. To covet deeply enough is to steal outright. Every pickpocket, every gangster, every knight of the road is, of course, covetous.

Not only may a covetous man become a liar, an adulterer, a trickster, and a thief; but again and again he becomes a murderer. A few days ago, a little chap just five years of age was sleeping quietly in his baby bed down in Princeton, Florida. A young man stole into the house, gathered this little chap into his arms, . . . and you know the rest of the fiendish story. What lay back of that ghastly deed? This villain did not kidnap and slay from anger. His deed was born of covetousness. It was covetousness that raped Ethiopia. It is this same cruel killer that is now seeking the conquest of China. The covetous man is often a man of soiled and bloody hands. The same is true of the group or the nation that gives way to this cruel passion.

3. But covetousness is a deadly thing, even though it leads to no deed of outward cruelty. It is an inner rottenness that destroys the taste for what is best. One day Jesus was preaching a marvelous sermon on the Holy Spirit. But there was one man in his audience that was not in the least interested. He wondered impatiently why the Master did not come

down to earth, and talk about something that really counted. At last he could stand it no longer. So he broke in with this word: "Speak to my brother that he divide the inheritance with me. Show your right to a place in the sun by putting money in my pocket." Then it was that Jesus said solemnly: "Take heed and beware of covetousness." It is a ghastly thing that tends to kill the appreciation of life's finer values. A millionaire died in our state just a few days ago. They sang at his funeral the song, "There's a Gold Mine in the Sky." Let us hope that the song was a slander. But, to the covetous, a heaven without gold mines would be no heaven at all.

Being thus a rottenness of the inner life, it shuts its possessor out of the kingdom. Twice over, Paul tells us that covetousness is a form of idolatry. The man who worships mammon naturally cannot worship God. The Apostle James declares that the covetous man, the man who puts the world first, is hostile to God. "The love of the world is enmity against God." "We know," says Paul, "that no covetous man, who is an idolater, hath any inheritance in the Kingdom of Christ and of God." Covetousness, then, makes fellowship with Jesus Christ an impossibility.

IV

How are we to conquer this deadly foe?

1. We can help ourselves to conquer covetousness by refusing to fix attention upon the forbidden. How much time we spend gazing upon values that we know we cannot have. I have known folk that could not go window-shopping without coming back fretful, discontented, and all but miserable. There were so many things that they wanted that they could not have that they felt quite sorry for themselves. Refuse to look longingly at that which you cannot have. That is good sense. It is also quite possible. More than once I have desired a thing intensely. But having found that it was not for me, I have ceased to look at it, and have thus forgotten it completely.

But how are we to do this? We are not to do it by merely closing our eyes. We are not to do it by saying, "I am not going to think of that something that is beyond my reach any more." Our one chance to forget the one object is by remembering another. We can forget the forbidden by looking at that which is legitimate. How did you forget the first man with whom you fell in love? How did you forget that first girl? The chances are that you did not do so by taking your love in your two hands and choking it to death. You forgot by falling in love with somebody else. In the conquering of covetousness, then, it will help to take one's gaze off that which is forbidden and fix it upon that which is permitted.

2. But since covetousness is a thing of the inner life, the supreme need is to be set right within. A sure way to victory, therefore, is the way of conversion. It is the way of the new-birth. It is the way of personal surrender to Jesus Christ. Paul, having put his life in the hands of his Lord, declared that it was God that worked within him, both to will and to do. That is, God enabled him to will what He himself willed. He enabled him to make right choices, and to have right desires. God enabled him to say from the inner depths of his soul, "Not my will, but Thine be done."

The issue of this was that Paul conquered covetousness. Thus conquering, he became a contented man. "I have learned," he says, "in whatsoever state I am, therewith to be content." What an achievement for one so passionate and hot-hearted! How did he attain? He did not win this contentment in a moment. He learned it through long discipline. He learned it, above all else, in the fellowship of Jesus Christ. And Paul's secret, I take it, is one that is well worth our learning. His was a type of contentment that, I am convinced, is at once the need and the desire of every discerning soul.

"I have learned in whatsoever state I am, therewith to be content." What did Paul mean by this? He did not mean that he was content with the world in which he lived, that he had become indifferent to its blindness, cruelty, and injustice. He was deeply concerned about his world. He declared that he had become all things to all men, if by any means he might save some. He even went so far as to say, "I catch myself wishing that I might be accursed from God, for my brethren, my kinsmen according to the flesh." No more was Paul contented with himself. "I am not perfect yet," he confesses. "But forgetting the things that are behind . . . , I press toward the mark of the prize."

If, then, Paul was contented neither with himself nor his world, in what sense was he contented? He was contented with the direction of his life. Though not satisfied with what he was, he was vastly contented with what he was becoming. Then he was contented with his work. He was thrilled by the fact that he was allowed to preach. He could never think of that privilege without a shout. "To me is this grace given that I might preach the unsearchable riches of Christ." Finally he was contented with his Master. He confesses that his pockets are empty, that his bank account has been wiped out. Yet, though possessing nothing, he still claims to possess all things.

The way of victory for Paul is the way of victory for you and me. I have a friend who is deeply learned in the things of God. He is not a man of the schools, yet his labors have been so abundant as to put most of us to shame. Uneducated himself, he has educated almost a hundred young men for the ministry. Some time ago this rare saint took a little vacation. He went to New York and spent one whole day sight-seeing in that glamorous city. When the exciting and joyous day was over he made his way, late at night, back to his hotel. He went to his room, bowed beside his bed, and prayed this prayer: "Lord, I want to thank you that I have not seen a single thing that I want." This man has learned in the fellowship of Jesus how to conquer covetousness. By so doing, he has also learned one of the greatest secrets of contentment and peace.

XI

THE SUPREME RULE

This is the first and great commandment

MATTHEW 22: 38

I

A CERTAIN LAWYER HAS JUST ASKED JESUS A question. His question was not asked in complete sincerity. He was asking to test the knowledge of Jesus rather than to gain knowledge for himself. But what his question lacked in sincerity was atoned for, in some measure, by its sanity and good sense. The Jews were a people of many rules. They had hundreds of them. There were in all more than six hundred. This lawyer is asking a question that must have perplexed every man who took these rules seriously. He is asking which one of them is most important, which is fundamental. To this question asked in insincerity, Jesus gives a sane and sincere answer.

What is his answer? What, amidst this maddening maze of rules, is really essential? Love is the answer. Love to God and love to man. We are to do as we please so long as our lives are motivated by love. This rule of love to God and man is not really two rules, but one. Love to God and love to man are two parts of a single whole. In the nature of things they belong together. We cannot divide them except at our peril. "What God hath joined together, let no man put asunder." Different generations have put different emphases upon the two parts of this rule. One has put the emphasis upon love to God, another upon love to man. But if we are wise we shall give emphasis to both.

1. We are to love God. This is essential to an adequate and intelligent love for man. I am not forgetting that there have been men here and there who have had a real passion for humanity who have reckoned without God. But these are exceptions rather than the rule. Faith in God is essential to an adequate appreciation of man. If we reckon without God, then man is too insignificant to love. If he is a product of blind chance; if he, as some describe him, is only a parasite on the epidermis of a

midge planet; if he is only a monkey digging for ground nuts while he chatters of his kinship with the archangels; then he is too contemptible to love. But if he is really a child of God, if he is an object of redemption, if he is a citizen of eternity, then he is capable of being loved. Then we can indeed see in every man a brother for whom Christ died. But if we leave God out of the picture, man loses all his significance.

2. We are to love man. As love to man falls far short without love to God, so love to God is an impossibility without love to man. The pious Jews in Jesus' day put the emphasis on love to God. For man, at least for a certain type of man, they possessed an indifference that often issued in a profound contempt. It was to rebuke this attitude that Jesus told the story of a certain rich man who was clothed in purple and fine linen and had a banquet every day. In fact, he got so busy entertaining himself and those of his own class that he failed to see a beggar that was dying of want at his very gate. Therefore, one day this professed lover of God hung his toes in the rags of that old beggar and fell flat into perdition. He made the mistake of thinking he could love God without loving man.

But there can be no love to God without love to

man. "If we love not our brother whom we have seen," asks the Apostle with fine common sense, "how can we love God whom we have not seen?" The Master gave one plain test of discipleship. What is that test? He showed that discipleship is not a mere matter of creed. It is not a matter of denominational affiliation. It is not a matter of how one is baptized. It goes far beyond all this. "By this," He declares, "shall all men know that ye are my disciples, if ye have love one toward another." Therefore, to claim to love God while we are indifferent or antagonistic to our fellows is to make of our religion an utter futility. There is, then, just one essential rule for living. That is to love God with an undivided heart, and to love one's neighbor as one's self. Love to God and love to man.

II

Now what is it thus to love God and man? In other words, what do we mean by love?

Love is a word that tends to become tarnished and emptied of all high meaning. It is something more than a shallow sentiment. It is something far finer than a wild dream of pleasures or a madness of desire. It is something far purer than the mere glamour with which we often seek to glorify lust. One half-serious humorist has described love as an "inexpressible all-overness," but it goes infinite distances beyond all this. To love, in the sense in which Jesus uses the word, is something unspeakably big and beautiful.

What, then, does it mean to love? First, what is it to love God? It is something far more significant than a mere emotional fondness. To love God is to obey him. "He that hath my commandments and keepeth them, he it is that loveth me." To love God is to enter into friendship with Him. "Ye are my friends if ye do whatsoever I command you." Friendship has two sides. If God is my friend, that means that he stoops to my interests. There is not a legitimate interest of my life that does not concern Him. He is interested in my task, my loved ones, my home. He is interested in every interest of my life. This is the case because he is my friend.

But if the Lord stoops to my interests, then, if I am to be his friend, I must rise to his interests. Is he interested in my church? He is. Then I must be interested in it. Is he interested in other churches? He is. Then I must be interested in them. Is he interested in the multitudes that are without the church? Then I must be interested in these multitudes. Is he interested in the folks that are white? Then I must be interested in them. Is he interested in the races of color? Then I must be interested in them. I may begin as a disciple with narrow interests. But if I am to be God's friend in the fullest sense, I must come to have a map of the world upon my heart. God's objectives must become my objectives. To love God, then, is to obey him. It is to be loyal to him. It is to make his plans and purposes for the world my very own.

And what is it to love man? This, too, is more than a sentimental fondness. To love our fellows, in a Christian sense, does not mean that we enjoy the companionship of one just as much as that of another. I used to teach school. Now and then I heard my fellow teachers boast of the fact that they had no favorites, that they loved all of their students equally well. But I doubt if this is ever the case. The best that any teacher can do is to be fair and impartial, regardless of likes or dislikes. The teacher that really does love every pupil in the same fashion does not genuinely love any of them at all. The man who professes an indiscriminate love for humanity is very likely not to care for any individual. He is like the cynic who delared that he could love humanity if it were not for folks.

To love in the Christian sense is to be possessed of good will toward men. This good will is something far finer than a cheap and bloodless wishing well to one's fellows. It is an active, aggressive, and sacrificial something. It is a power that, getting into our heart, makes it so beat as to break the lock off our own front door, and the latch off our own front gate. It is a dynamic something that sends one out to share the burdens and needs of a broken world. It is a thing of such might that it bridges all chasms. It even bridges that wide chasm between ourselves and our enemies; between ourselves and those that despitefully use us and persecute us.

About three years ago a friend introduced me to a rather insignificant-looking college professor. But I saw him through different eyes when my friend told me his story. This teacher had come originally from Germany. During the World War he undertook to be a Christian. That, of course, was exceedingly difficult, and got him into trouble. He was accused of being a German sympathizer. One night a company of men went to his house and arrested him. They took him to a certain hall, put a German flag into his hand, and ordered him to spit upon it. But, to their amazement, he refused. "You will either do as you have been ordered," he was told, "or we are going to hang you from that window. Not only so, but your wife is going to be brought to witness the execution."

That was plain enough. What did this defenseless Christian have to say? He looked at his captors with quiet eyes and said, "Your action will be regrettable. But I cannot do your bidding. You cannot make me hate the German people any more than you can make me hate yourselves. Whatever happens, whether I live or die, I expect to do so with good will in my heart toward you and toward all my fellows." That is Christian love. It is the same kind of love of which Peter was thinking when he wrote of infinitely the most amazing Man he had ever known. And what amazed him most was this: "When he was reviled, he reviled not again." To love then in a Christian sense, is to be possessed of an active, sacrificial, and invincible good will.

III

WE can begin to see why to love in this fashion is the supreme achievement. We can understand how Drummond is only following his Master when he calls this love the greatest thing in the world. Why is this the case?

1. Love is supreme because nothing really arrives

without it. "Though I speak with the tongues of men and of angels, and have not love, I am become as sounding brass, or a tinkling cymbal. And though I have the gift of prophecy, and understand all mysteries, and all knowledge; and though I have all faith, so that I could remove mountains, and have not love, I am nothing. And though I bestow all my goods to feed the poor, and though I give my body to be burned, and have not love, it profiteth me nothing." "Nothing," declares Paul, "ever arrives without love," not giving to the point of utter impoverishment, not even sacrificing to the point of laying down one's life.

Really, that sounds a bit harsh till we realize we are close enough kin to God to feel just as he feels. Nothing arrives with us without love. The other day a man did you what you thought was a beautiful courtesy. But something happened a bit later that forced you to the conviction that he was not so much seeking to serve you as he was seeking to use you. At once his courtesy lost all its beauty. Here is a lovely girl. A man, young, attractive, fascinating, shows her costly and captivating attentions. But this girl finds that his motives, instead of being high and holy, are base and sordid. What is the result? Even his loveliest flowers, sent under such circumstances, become nothing better than noxious weeds. With us, as with God, nothing counts unless it is motivated by love.

2. Then love is supreme because, while nothing counts without it, the least thing is of value when transformed by it. Even the giving of a cup of cold water becomes a priceless service. A handclasp or a smile often becomes a treasure more precious than gold. Jesus told of a certain widow who once made an offering that was so insignificant as to seem to some positively disgraceful. She gave only about three mills. Yet Jesus was wildly enthusiastic about that gift. There were many rich men present, and they gave freely. But the Master declared that this widow had given more than all the others together. Why was this the case? The others gave money, and little else. But this woman gave two mites plus her whole heart's love. Love then is the supreme thing because nothing arrives without it, and the least thing is priceless with it.

3. Then love is supreme because it fulfills the law. This it does both negatively and positively. In the language of Paul, "Love worketh no ill to his neighbor." If we love our fellows we are not going to bear false witness against them. If we love them, we are not going to take advantage of them. We

are not going to steal from them, either within or without the law. If we love, we are not going to kill. Love builds a wall of defense around every human life. If we love our fellows, we will not knowingly do them harm of any kind.

But love not only fulfills the law by doing no harm; it fulfills it by doing every possible good. Love is that springtime of the soul that must give expression to itself in deeds of service. God cannot hide springtime in that bit of earth in the back yard, and expect it to keep it a secret. It will tell the world. It will tell through the green of the grass and through the color and perfume of the flowers. And this springtime of love, once it gets into a human heart, must also express itself. Love is restless and inventive. It will do the big thing if possible. If not, it will do the small thing grandly. It will beautify a palace if it has an opportunity. If not, it will transform a cottage. Love thus fulfills the law, not only by working no ill, but by doing every possible good.

4. Finally, love is supreme because it is the mightiest force on earth. It sends men on the most heroic and daring missions. It keeps them at their post when nothing else will. It even has power to change indifference into friendship. It has power to change

hate into love. And that, I take it, is the most amazing power in all the world. I have actually had its efficacy tried upon myself. Some years ago I went to a city where a man lived whom I knew by reputation, and against whom I had a profound prejudice. This man is my friend today, and it is all his doing. He killed my prejudice, and changed my dislike into friendship. This he did in the sanest and simplest way possible. He did it by an invincible good will.

As a further proof of its power, let me now finish the story of the college professor that we left looking death eye to eye. What happened when he told his tormenters that they could hang him if they would; but that they could not make him hate either them or anyone else? This happened: a big broad-shouldered chap stood up in their midst and said, "You can't hang this man. That is, you cannot hang him unless you hang me with him." And the professor was allowed to go without a scratch. What had happened? Love had put its transforming hands upon hate and changed it into its own glorious image. And of all the victories of love, this is surely the greatest, that it has skill beyond all else, to change hate into love.

IV

How, then, shall we keep this first and great command? This is, of course, the most important question for every single one of us. Other things may matter, but nothing matters so much as this. In answer to this question, I have to say four very simple words.

1. Believe in love. There is nothing more evident than that Jesus staked everything on his faith in the final victory of good will. It is not always easy for us to follow him in this. We are prone to pin our faith to force, to well-organized armies, to big navies. We are prone to forget that hate only begets hate, that he that taketh the sword shall perish with the sword. If we share the faith of Jesus, we must believe that the final victory is not to be with hate, but with love.

2. Realize love. When a man becomes really convinced of the love of one of his fellows, that realization makes his own love spontaneous. Here, for instance, is a cross-grained individual who gets onto your nerves. But one day a friend tells you a beautiful compliment. "Who said that kind word?" you ask. And your friend tells you that it was this cross-grained chap. And, lo, a miracle takes place. Love tends to blossom in your heart

as naturally as violets bloom at the kiss of spring. Thus also we come to love God." "We love Him," says the Apostle, "because He first loved us." And when Paul accounts for his own deathless passion for his Lord, he does it in this fashion: "He loved me and gave himself up for me." As a help to love, then, realize love, the love of your fellows and the love of your Lord.

3. Express love. Suppose you go out tomorrow to act toward all your fellows as if you really love them. What would happen? Even though your love might be small to begin with, as you should express it, it would grow from more to more. We naturally love those who help us, who comfort us in our sorrows and reach a hand to us in our need. But I dare say that we love even more those whom we serve in such fashion. There is something about living sacrificially for others that makes them very dear. This accounts for the fact that the mother usually loves best the child for whom she has to make the greatest sacrifice. That also is one reason why it is more blessed to give than to receive. Express the love you have, and it will grow from more to more.

4. Finally, receive love. "Behold I stand at the door and knock." Who is it knocking? It is Love.

If you open the door, you will come to share the nature of Him whose name is Love. Sometime ago I was preaching in a backwoods community. At the close of the service I invited anyone interested in becoming a Christian for a personal word. In response to my invitation two men came. One was a cultured man from one of our best colleges. The other was obviously a roughneck. I approached the young college man first. This was my question, "Will you accept Jesus Christ if I tell you how?"

"Surely I will," was the response. "That is what I am here for." Then I explained to him the best I could what it meant to become a Christian. "Is that all?" he asked, when I had finished.

"That is all you need to begin," I replied.

"All right," he said, "I accept." Then what happened? He did not shout. He did not burst into song. But he did something far more significant. He turned at once, put his arm about the roughneck at his side, and said, "Let me tell you how to become a Christian." If you want to get hold on love, get hold on God, for "God is love."